Painting and Sculpture in Minnesota, 1820–1914

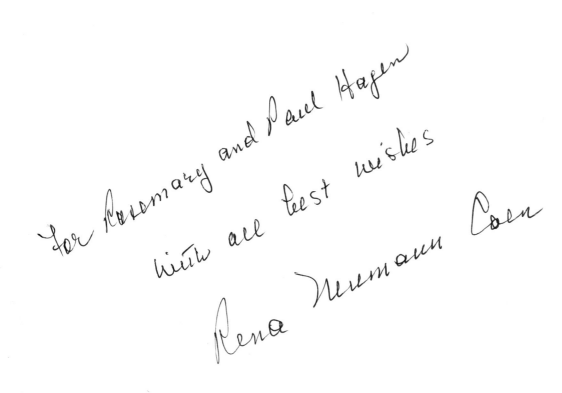

For Rosemary and Paul Hagen
with all best wishes

Rena Neumann Coen

Painting and Sculpture in Minnesota 1820-1914

RENA NEUMANN COEN

Published by the University of Minnesota Press, Minneapolis,
for the University Gallery of the University of Minnesota

Copyright © 1976 by the University of Minnesota
All rights reserved. Printed in the United States of America
at Harrison-Smith, Lund Press, Minneapolis
Published in Canada by Burns & MacEachern Limited,
Don Mills, Ontario

Library of Congress Catalog Card Number 75-27788
ISBN 0-8166-0771-0

Contents

Black and White Illustrations

Color Illustrations

Foreword

Minnesota is recognized for the talented artists, designers, craftsmen, and architects who have lived and worked here. These creative men and women have produced an outstanding cultural environment that is a major contributor to our high quality of life.

Awareness and appreciation of the arts have also been characteristic of Minnesotans. Painting, sculpture, historic buildings, and minor arts as well are treasured as a record of our people.

Painting and Sculpture in Minnesota, 1820–1914 represents the best of both these traditions. The book preserves the outstanding artistic heritage of our state for future generations. Perhaps this record will stimulate more research into the depth, originality, and vitality of Minnesota art. If so, it will come at a time when Minnesotans are becoming increasingly aware of the need to preserve our state's art treasures.

I am particularly pleased that *Painting and Sculpture in Minnesota, 1820–1914* is being published in America's Bicentennial year. An understanding of regional art and history enriches our appreciation of the national story. I can think of no more appropriate way to recognize the 200th anniversary of the birth of this great nation.

Wendell R. Anderson
Governor of Minnesota

Background Note

Painting and Sculpture in Minnesota, 1820–1914 is a book with a dual purpose. In addition to being, to our knowledge, the first study of the art of our state considered in depth and within the context of American art history, it also serves as a catalogue for one of the components of the University Gallery's major Bicentennial exhibition, *The Art and Architecture of Minnesota*. The other components of the exhibition were organized to depict Minnesota's architectural history from the beginning of white settlement to the present day and to display the Indian arts of the state. When we began our plans more than two and one-half years ago for an exhibition of this uncharted field, a conventional exhibition catalogue seemed appropriate to our needs. But as our knowledge deepened and the abysmal lack of information on the subject became apparent, we found that initial plan inadequate and a simple catalogue far too ephemeral. We wanted a more permanent record of art in our state as a reference for future generations of Minnesotans, the "enjoyers" as well as the students and scholars. Therefore a book, properly published by the state's University Press, appeared to be the most suitable form for the research to take. An important bonus is that we could go beyond the exhibition itself. Thus, one important problem was solved, for with only a catalogue what would we have done with "the ones that got away"? An exhibition catalogue is only a record of the objects on display for the run of a particular show, and every show has its disappointments — the loan of certain objects is refused and they, therefore, cannot be included. Happily the book can make up for these omissions, and the author can here include a discussion of most of the important works which contribute to the history of art in Minnesota, a field intimately related to the broader one of American art history.

The author's discoveries include works now housed in such prestigious collections as those of the Peabody Museum of Harvard University and the national museum, the Smithsonian Institution, as well as works which for lack of proper exhibition space have for years been lodged in the basements of historical societies. These works, preserved as historic documents by their owners, have never been studied from the point of view of American art history and were frequently in a lamentable state of disrepair. A special grant from the Minnesota American Revolution Bicentennial Commission for their conservation and restoration was necessary not only to put them in exhibitable condition but even to permit adequate photography for exhibition purposes.

The conservation grant was the one bit of fundraising for this complex project which was the most difficult to achieve and the one about which we felt happiest. For without it there would literally have been no exhibition and no book. It was often difficult to convince potential funding agencies that underneath the accumulated dirt and grime of the years, beyond the rents and tears in the canvases, there was something worth preserving. Now that the alchemy of conservation has been performed and the works are restored to their original beauty and freshness, we hope that all will admire them and be convinced of the wisdom of our procedures. The grant from the Bicentennial Commission covered only works of art in public collections in Minnesota; for those from outside the state we are indebted to an additional, smaller grant from the Patrick and Aimée Butler Family Foundation. All Minnesotans owe the Commission and Foundation a debt of gratitude, for one of the nicest subsidiary aspects of this entire endeavor is that the works will now return to their lending institutions in superb condition, ready to be enjoyed by future generations of Americans.

In addition to the Minnesota American Revolution Bicentennial Commission, one other supporter of our total project should be singled out. The National Endowment for the Arts funded all the thousands of miles of travel throughout the country and the state which made the research for the book and exhibition a possibility. Further, two individuals believed in our project and in our ability to accomplish it before we had the opportunity to prove ourselves. We thus thank Ruth Humleker and Dean Myhr, then of the Minnesota State Arts Council, for their faith and their willingness to gamble. I am confident that Rena Coen's book alone will prove their judgment correct.

Barbara Shissler
Director,
University of Minnesota Gallery

Preface

This book, like the Bicentennial exhibition out of which it grew, begins with the establishment of Fort Snelling and ends in 1914. Though the cutoff date might seem arbitrary, it is meant to conform with the Smithsonian Institution's *Bicentennial Inventory of American Painting Executed before 1914.* The *Inventory* is a comprehensive directory of American painting from the earliest years of our national history to the present century. A less comprehensive, though similarly systematic, description of Minnesota's art is attempted in this book. Both it and the *Inventory* will serve as a record of the visual arts of the past, the former on a regional scale, the latter on a national one. It is hoped that in addition to helping preserve that past through public awareness of it, both works will also serve as research tools for scholars, connoisseurs, and just plain art lovers. The beginning of World War I, moreover, in the year after New York's Armory Show, can be used as the watershed between past and present, for after 1914 American art, while still retaining some regional characteristics, nevertheless became a full-fledged participant in the international art scene. It is, of course, greatly to be hoped that a future book — and exhibition — will carry the story forward to our own time.

Many devoted individuals helped to make the exhibition and the book possible. First I would like to thank Ellen W. Bauer, my associate throughout this project and my cheerful companion in exploring many dusty attics and crowded storerooms. Mrs. Bauer is also responsible for the Appendix of Minnesota artists at the end of the book. A large debt of gratitude is owed Marion J. Nelson, professor of art history at the University of Minnesota and director of the Norwegian-American Museum at Decorah, Iowa. Without his encouragement and generous help both the book and the exhibition would have been much the poorer. I have frequently turned to the work of Donald R. Torbert, professor of art history at the University of Minnesota, who was the first to write about the art of the state from the art historian's point of view. I am especially grateful to Barbara Shissler, director of the University of Minnesota Gallery, for supporting my two quarters' leaves of absence from St. Cloud State College, which provided me with the opportunity to organize the painting and sculpture portion of the Bicentennial exhibition and to write this book.

Others helped in ways too numerous to mention. Lyndel King, assistant director of the University of Minnesota Gallery, was generous with her time and good advice. I had encouraging support from staff members of many state and local historical societies and museums. Among them were Lila Goff and Bonnie Wilson of the Minnesota State Historical Society, Frank Young and David Vaughan of the St. Louis County Historical Society, Dr. Louis I. Younger, William Gernes, and Molly McGuire of the Winona County Historical Society, George Tyrell and Brad J. Linder of the Olmsted County Historical Museum, Leah Strandquist of the Roseau County Museum, Mrs. Frank Chesley of the Goodhue County Historical Society, and Ruth Thorstenson of the Hennepin County Historical Society. Gregory Hedberg, curator of paintings of the Minneapolis Institute of Arts, and Jamie Besso, a student intern at the Institute, were most helpful. I am grateful to Herbert Scherer and his staff at the Art Library of the University of Minnesota and to the library staff at the Minnesota Historical Society for patient assistance. Paul Kramer and Linnea Wren of St. Paul were also helpful. Helen M. White of Taylor's Falls brought to my attention several artists of that area. I drew on the resources of the Smithsonian Institution's *Bicentennial Inventory of American Painting Executed before 1914* and am grateful to Abigail Booth, its coordinator, for timely help. Mildred Goosman of the Joslyn Museum, Omaha, provided initial encouragement and continued assistance. I am indebted to Richard E. Kuehne, of the United States Military Academy Museum at West Point, and to William H. Gerdts and Lee Baxandall, both of New York City, who offered valuable suggestions. Nina and Louis Nidus of Lexington, Massachusetts, and Ethan Jesse of Great Barrington, Massachusetts, provided research help in Boston and Stockbridge, respectively. Peter Williams, of Hingham, Massachusetts, the conservator for the Minnesota Bicentennial exhibition, also offered good advice. Susan Brown read the manuscript and suggested improvements in style and exposition. Rita DuCharme-Kachhal typed and retyped the manuscript and Mary Hofstadter pleasantly and efficiently provided office assistance. I hope this book will be a small token of my gratitude to all of them.

Rena Neumann Coen

Minneapolis, June 1975

Painting and Sculpture in Minnesota, 1820–1914

A Note on Illustrations

In all measurements, height precedes width.
Dimensions for figures 64, 86, 87, 88, 89, 90, 92, and
102 are unavailable.

Plate 1. Peter Rindisbacher. *Inside an Indian Tent*. Cambridge, Mass. Courtesy of
Peabody Museum of Archaeology and Ethnology, Harvard University.
Water color, 8⅜ x 10¼ inches.

Plate 2. George Catlin. *Sioux Hunters Pursuing a Stag in the St. Peter's River*, 1835. Washington, D.C. Courtesy of National Collection of Fine Arts, Smithsonian Institution. Oil on canvas, 19½ x 27⅝ inches.

Plate 3. George Catlin. *Pipestone Quarry on the Coteau des Prairies,*
1836. Washington, D.C. Courtesy of National Collection
of Fine Arts, Smithsonian Institution. Oil
on canvas, 19½ x 27⅞ inches.

Plate 4.
Attributed to George Catlin.
Portrait of Colonel Lawrence Taliaferro.
St. Paul. Courtesy of Minnesota Historical Society.
Oil on canvas, 42 x 35 inches.

Plate 5. Charles Deas. *View of Fort Snelling*, 1841. Cambridge, Mass. Courtesy of
Peabody Museum of Archaeology and Ethnology, Harvard University.
Oil on canvas, 12 x 14½ inches.

Plate 6. Seth Eastman. *Indian on the Lookout*. Omaha. Courtesy of Joslyn Museum
of Art. Collection of Northern Natural Gas Company.
Oil on canvas, 29¾ x 22 inches.

Plate 7. Sergeant Edward K. Thomas. *View of Fort Snelling*, c. 1850. Minneapolis.
Courtesy of The Minneapolis Institute of Arts. The Julia B. Bigelow Fund.
Oil on canvas, 27 x 34 inches.

Plate 8. John Caspar Wild. *View of Ft. Snelling*, 1844. St. Paul. Courtesy of Minnesota Historical Society. Water color and gouache, 20 x 30 inches.

Plate 9. Henry Lewis. *The Gorge of the St. Croix*, 1847. Minneapolis. Courtesy of The
Minneapolis Institute of Arts. The Julia B. Bigelow Fund. Oil on canvas, 20 x 30 inches.

Plate 10. Henry Lewis. *St. Anthony Falls as It Appeared in 1848*, 1855. Minneapolis.
Courtesy of The Minneapolis Institute of Arts. Gift of Mr. E. C. Gale.
Oil on canvas, 19 x 27 inches.

Plate 11.
Eastman Johnson. *Minnesota Point*, 1856.
St. Paul. Collection
of Michael Jaglowski. Oil
on canvas, 12½ x 18½ inches.

Plate 12.
Eastman Johnson. *Portrait of Hiawatha*.
Duluth. Courtesy of St. Louis
County Historical Society.
Pastel, 13½ x 11 inches.

Plate 13. John Kensett. *View on the Upper Mississippi.* St. Louis. Courtesy of St. Louis City Art Museum. Oil on canvas, 18⅜ x 30¼ inches.

Plate 14. Albert Bierstadt. *View of Duluth*. Duluth. Collection of
Jeno and Lois Paulucci. Oil on canvas, 27½ x 34¼ inches.

Plate 15. Robert Duncanson. *The Falls of Minnehaha*, 1862. London. Courtesy of
Richard Green (Fine Paintings). Oil on canvas, 36 x 28 inches.

Plate 16. Thomas P. Rossiter. *Minnesota Prairie*, 1865. Minneapolis. Courtesy of
University of Minnesota Gallery. Oil on canvas, 14 x 24 inches.

Plate 17.
Thomas Waterman Wood. *Little Crow*, 1862.
Minneapolis. Courtesy of The
Minneapolis Institute of Arts.
Oil on canvas, 30 x 25 inches.

Plate 18.
Edwin Whitefield. *First View of
Fairy Lake*, 1857. St. Paul. Courtesy
of Minnesota Historical Society.
Water color, 5½ x 8½ inches.

Plate 19. S. J. Durran. *Sunday Afternoon on the Levee*, 1895. Winona. Courtesy of
Winona County Historical Society. Oil on canvas, 22 x 30 inches.

Introduction

When the Minnesota Territory became the thirty-second state in 1858, it already had a history of accomplishment in the visual arts. As early, in fact, as the first military expeditions that were sent to explore the upper reaches of the great river that divided the country, artists were recording the appearance of the new territory and making it known to an interested eastern public. For in the early days of western exploration, and before the perfection of the camera as a journalistic tool, the artist's pen and brush were the only means of visually describing the wide and fertile river-fed valley that later became the state of Minnesota.

There were a number of such artist-explorers in the Minnesota Territory, for the lure of adventuring into the unknown was as attractive to them as it was to trailblazers of different talents. George Catlin is the best known but not the only footloose wanderer to have traveled through the area in its early days, and his descriptions, both written and painted, are valuable sources of our knowledge of Indian life in the 1830's. Even earlier than Catlin, the explorer Jonathan Carver visited the upper Mississippi in 1767, and though he was not an artist, he made a sketch of the Falls of St. Anthony to illustrate the account of his travels. About fifty years later, in 1823, when the map-making expedition of Major Stephen H. Long was sent to find the source of the St. Peter's (now Minnesota) River, it was accompanied by a "zoologist, an antiquary and a landscape painter."[1]

Even while explorers were still mapping the new lands, artists of more settled habits were to be found among the soldiers stationed in the frontier outposts as well as among the settlers themselves. Peter Rindisbacher, a Swiss-born artist who painted scenes in northern Minnesota as early as the 1820's, was the first to record Chippewa life and the flora and fauna of the area. Captain Seth Eastman at Fort Snelling also sketched Indian life in Minnesota and later translated those sketches into monumental paintings which were bought by the United States Congress. About 1850 Sergeant Edward K. Thomas, an obscure soldier and probably self-taught artist from Philadelphia, built up a cottage industry painting views of Fort Snelling which he did while stationed there and sold as prizes of lotteries advertised in the local press. Others, whose names and works are lost today, also drew, sketched, and painted either to entertain themselves in an idle moment or to pursue the practice of art as a serious profession.

Some of these recorders of the early Minnesota scene eventually established independent reputations as important American artists of the nineteenth century, Catlin and Eastman among them. But there were others, men such as Henry Lewis, whose reputations did not survive them though they were well known and much admired in their own day. Nor does much remain of their work, which in Lewis's case included a large panorama of the Mississippi River from its source in northern Minnesota to the Gulf. The panorama, which will be discussed more fully later on, was an art form unique to the nineteenth century and particularly favored by artists of the Mississippi River Valley who sought to capture on large continuous rolls of canvas the power and majesty of the famous river.

Least known of all, of course, were the folk artists who were frequently anonymous, who had little or no academic training, who labored humbly in the artistic vineyard, and who died in the same obscurity in which they had lived and worked. These artists, "primitives" in varying degree, produced naive portraits of their friends and relations, landscapes, frequently fanciful, for their own or their neighbors' enjoyment, and carved or painted altarpieces for their churches. For these people, art was usually an activity of their leisure hours and not the means by which they earned their living. The avocational aspect of their art is one criterion separating their work from that of the professional.

Besides the professional artists who became Minnesota settlers, others, though not residents of the state, nevertheless had an important role to play in its art history. These were the eastern painters who, from the middle of the nineteenth century to its end, embarked on leisurely sketching expeditions in search of new and "picturesque" subjects for paintings they would finish in their studios back home. The Mississippi River, the bluffs near Winona, and, above all, Minnehaha Falls were the main attractions for these itinerant, usually summer, visitors. Albert Bierstadt and John Kensett were among them, though many others, less well known, also took the slow steamboat trip up the Mississippi River with sketchbook and pencil in hand. These traveling artists are particularly important not only for their vivid pictorial record of the Minnesota of over a hundred years ago, but also because of the significant link they provide to the mainstream of what has aptly been called the American tradition in art. For these men, influenced though they were by the conventions of European painting (from which, ultimately, American art is derived), nevertheless reflect in attitude, in subject matter, and, to a certain extent, even in style those qualities which we define as peculiarly and typically American.

Toward the end of the nineteenth century, there began to emerge a number of painters and sculptors to whom the term "Minnesota artists" might properly be applied. Prominent in this group are Alexis Fournier, Douglas Volk, and Robert Koehler, the last two of whom were early directors of the Minneapolis School of Art (today the Minneapolis College of Art and Design). These men are attracting renewed interest today as important long-neglected artists, especially Koehler, who is now being recognized as a pioneer of social protest in American painting.

Others, too, by the beginning of the twentieth century were working professionally and making their home in the state. They came from widely different cultural and ethnic backgrounds. Some came as immigrants. Some arrived from the eastern seaboard and some were even born in Minnesota. The painting and sculpture they produced is the subject of this book. This is not, however, an exhaustive account of every artist who worked in the area from the first white settlement to 1914. It is, rather, an attempt to describe American art of the nineteenth and early twentieth century from a Minnesota point of view. The art produced in the state was not, of course, an isolated phenomenon. There is, after all, no such thing as a "Minnesota style." But there is an art that has a strong and self-apparent Minnesota focus and that constitutes a small but important aspect of the wider story of American artistic life. For the art of this nation is more than the sum of its many regional parts, as each region reflects both national cultural trends and its own local history. The tie that binds, then, is neither a definable style nor even a characteristic attitude but a tenuous, though real, sense of shared experience—an identification, however fleeting, with the Minnesota scene.

I Explorers

Our story properly begins in the 1820's when Minnesota was still very much a frontier territory. Fort Snelling, at the confluence of the Mississippi and Minnesota rivers, had barely been established as a military outpost to adjudicate recurring quarrels among the Indians, to encourage and protect the fur trade, and to protect the land-hungry immigrants, who, in their eagerness to establish a claim of their own, were pushing America's frontier ever westward.

Samuel Seymour (1796–1823), who accompanied Major Stephen H. Long's exploring expedition to the Minnesota Territory in 1823, is probably the first artist to have come to this area with the deliberate intention of painting its landscape and its native inhabitants.[1] Little is known about him except that he was born in England and that by 1801 he was working as a painter and engraver in Philadelphia. He must have maintained a home in that city, for after his death his works were exhibited there at Peale's Museum in 1832. Yale University's Collection of Western Americana contains a number of Seymour's water colors, all of them, however, of areas further south and west. Though he is known to have painted a number of Minnesota scenes, including one of Maiden Rock[2] (from which Wenonah is said to have leaped to her death in the Mississippi River), only one of these survives. It is a small water color, carefully and minutely drawn, depicting an Indian encampment at Big Stone Lake, head of the St. Peter.[3] It probably dates from 1823, the year of the Long expedition, and was meant to describe what the photojournalist's camera would have recorded in a later day.

James Otto Lewis (1799–1858), another artist-explorer, was also from Philadelphia, a city that was, incidentally, a center of culture and the arts in the United States in the early part of the nineteenth century. Lewis was sent as an artist-member of the expedition of Lewis Cass, governor of the Michigan Territory, to paint the Indians at the 1825 Treaty of Prairie du Chien at Fort Crawford, Fort Snelling's closest neighbor to the east. Lewis's portraits were later destroyed in a disastrous fire at the Smithsonian Institution, but copies of his work may be seen in his well-known collection *The Aboriginal Portfolio*, published in 1835. While at Fort Crawford Lewis also sketched Maiden Rock, near present-day Winona, but Lewis's sketch, like so much of Seymour's work, has unfortunately disappeared.

A better known artist, many of whose works fortunately do survive, is Peter Rindisbacher (1806–1834), whose images of the American Indian were enormously influential in later artists' portrayals of the native inhabitants of the West. Rindisbacher was born in the canton of Berne, Switzerland. In 1821, at the age of fifteen, he immigrated with his parents to the remote and primitive Red River colony that had been established by Lord Selkirk some years earlier near present-day Winnipeg. During his twelfth summer, Peter had wandered through the Alps under the tutorial supervision of the Bernese painter Jacob S. Weibel, and this seems to have been the extent of his artistic training. Weibel's careful miniature portraits and detailed landscapes left a lasting impression on his young pupil's mind. They are reflected in the painstaking drawing and tidy realism with which Rindisbacher later represented the colorful Indian life around him. In spite of his dry and meticulous style, Rindisbacher's work has an immediacy, a feeling of closeness to his subjects, that leads one to believe that he had easy access to the lodges of the Chippewa, Cree, Assiniboin, and Eastern Sioux of the Manitoba and Minnesota territories (see plate 1). He painted their villages, their mode of travel, their ceremonies, and even their quarrels with each other and with the white man. Above all he painted the buffalo hunts, upon which Plains Indian life depended (see fig. 1). Indeed, Rindisbacher's portrayal of the Indian as a skilled and daring buffalo hunter established a popular iconographic theme in American painting, an image of the West that ultimately became a visual metaphor for the decline of the buffalo and, by implication, the end of Indian life as well.[4]

Rindisbacher was just beginning to attract popular attention through lithographic reproduction of his work in *The American Turf Register and Sporting Magazine* when, at the very threshold of a blossoming career, he died suddenly in St. Louis at the age of twenty-eight. Though he was forgotten soon after his death—and has only recently aroused renewed interest as a significant painter of the early West—he was much admired in the rude frontier communities in which he lived. Two days after he died on August 13, 1834, an unknown correspondent mourned his passing in an obituary ode published in the *Missouri Republican.*

> No more for him the scenes he loved so well
> Will gleam in beauty on the ravished sight

> The woodland's shade—the prairie's sunny swell
> The glowing noontide—and the solemn night.

> No more will these or aught of nature's store,
> With joy; to Genius known his busom [*sic*] fill
> The heartfelt throb—the flush his high brow o'er
> The blood's quick rush—the fitful pleasing thrill!

> All's quiet now! Calm passionless and cold!
> But the warm heart's poor tenant's upward fled;
> In brighter scenes to taste of joy, untold
> And join the circle of th'illustrious dead.

By far the best known of the artist-explorers who visited the Minnesota Territory in its earliest years of white history was George Catlin (1796–1872), who made it his lifework to record North American Indian life. During the 1830's, he traveled extensively throughout the West and Southwest sketching and painting forty-eight Indian nations, in order, as he himself wrote, "to rescue from a hasty oblivion a truly noble and lofty race."[5] Catlin's nearly five hundred paintings are an almost complete record of "the living manners, customs and character" of the Indians, and his contribution to American anthropology is further assured by the book he wrote about them. This book was one of the first to study Indian cultures from a serious ethnological point of view and not merely as quaint curiosities in a wild and savage land. Indeed, Catlin's considerable sympathy for the Indians and his perceptive awareness of their plight is more explicitly described in his published work than in his hasty, impressionistic paintings of them. Thus, though he wrote of the "melancholy fact" of the imminent destruction of Plains Indians' life and drew "the irresistible conclusion that the buffalo is soon to be extinguished and with it the peace and happiness (if not the actual existence) of the tribes of Indians who are joint tenants with them in the occupancy of these vast and idle plains,"[6] his *Sioux Indians Hunting Buffalo* (fig. 2), painted in 1832, evokes an entirely different response. The quickness of the sketch seems to echo the quickly shifting scene as the frightened animals stampede across the picture plane and the Indians, displaying their legendary skill and daring, pursue them bareback on their swift horses. Even the sharp slope of

Fig. 1. Peter Rindisbacher. *Hunting Bison*. West Point, N.Y. Courtesy of West Point Museum Collections, United States Military Academy. Water color, 9 x 15¼ inches.

Fig. 2.
George Catlin. *Sioux Indians Hunting Buffalo*, 1832. New York. Courtesy of American Museum of Natural History. Oil on board, 18⅛ x 24¾ inches.

the hill in the background heightens the suggestion of speed and shifting movement. The same dash and spontaneity, so typical of Catlin's portrayal of the Indian, are to be seen in *Sioux Hunters Pursuing a Stag in the St. Peter's River* (plate 2), painted in the summer of 1835. Here too the sparkle and freshness of the painting may seem antithetical to the artist's somber written reflections. But the very quickness and sketchiness of his Indian paintings suggest the urgency with which Catlin felt compelled to record as much as he could of Indian life "in all its primitive rudeness" before Indian and buffalo, ". . . fugitives together from the approach of civilized man, will flee to the Great Plains of the West and there . . . take up their last abode where their race will expire and their bones bleach together."[7]

In the following summer of 1836 Catlin, in the company of Robert Serrill Wood, a traveling Englishman, visited the Pipestone quarry located in what is now southwestern Minnesota. The quarry's distinctive soft reddish stone, used by the Indians for peace pipes, was later named Catlinite in honor of the painter who,

because of his evident enthusiasm for all details of Indian life, was the first white man permitted access to this sacred Indian ground. His painting of the quarry (plate 3), in a loose and sketchy style, deftly conveys the expanse of the sacred Indian place and its remoteness from settled territory. It evokes, in fact, a quite different response from the genre picture of everyday life represented in *Village near the Falls of St. Anthony* (fig. 3) painted the year before.

It is interesting that when Catlin painted the portraits of white men his brush seems to have become suddenly inhibited, in startling contrast to the freer, looser brushwork evident in either his landscapes or such Indian portraits as *Blue Medicine*, depicting an Eastern Sioux medicine man (fig. 4). Catlin's usual white sitters were the Indian agents of the western territories, with whom he maintained many close friendships. It is entirely possible, therefore, that he painted the unsigned portrait of Major Lawrence Taliaferro (plate 4), Indian agent at the St. Peter's (Fort Snelling) Agency from 1820 to 1839. Though the effect of the Taliaferro portrait is less sketchy, less spontaneous,

Fig. 3. George Catlin. *Village near the Falls of St. Anthony* (Ojibway), 1835.
New York. Courtesy of American Museum of Natural History.
Oil on board, 18⅛ x 24¾ inches.

Fig. 4. George Catlin. *Blue Medicine*. Washington, D.C.
Courtesy of National Collection of Fine Arts,
Smithsonian Institution. Oil on canvas, 29 x 24 inches.

than the shorthand style he adopted for his Indian ones, it is similar to a Catlin portrait of General William Clark (Meriwether Lewis's colleague in the famous expedition of 1804–1806 from St. Louis to the Pacific and back), who was superintendent of Indian affairs in St. Louis in the 1830's. It is even more closely related to a Catlin portrait of Major Benjamin O'Fallon, Indian agent for the Upper Missouri Agency and therefore Taliaferro's closest colleague to the south.[8] We know, moreover, that Taliaferro in his daily journal and Catlin in his book[9] expressed an admiration for each other's work. It is only reasonable to assume that Taliaferro, who we know was a rather vain man, sat for Catlin during the latter's longer visit to the St. Peter's Agency in the summer of 1835. And if, as in the other white men's portraits by this artist, the one of Taliaferro reveals a harder line, a smoother finish, and a more labored technique than in the Indian portraits, the reason for this different treatment must be sought in Catlin's attitude toward the native red man. Like many other nineteenth-century artists (and writers too), he regarded the Indian as a "noble savage," Rousseau's child of nature, "undisguised and unfettered by the disguises of art and surely the most beautiful model for the painter."[10] Such sentiments may help to explain Catlin's apparent constraints and inhibited style in depicting the representatives of the white civilization that nearly destroyed the native Indian one.

One other interesting observation on Catlin's attitude toward his world is that, except for miniatures of his wife and mother, there are no known portraits by him of white women. When Major Taliaferro's wife, Elizabeth Dillon Taliaferro, wanted her portrait painted, she turned elsewhere. Her portrait (fig. 5) is a typical provincial image of a proper nineteenth-century lady of quality. Unlike the portrait of her husband, it makes no reference to her presence at a western fort, for white women, though frequently living at frontier outposts, were an anomaly at such establishments. Their role in the early nineteenth century was that of carefully protected, rather delicate creatures whose beauty would not survive a harsh and dangerous environment. So Mrs. Taliaferro's image is set against the background of an ideal landscape. She appears carefully coiffed, wearing a green silk scarf and an intricately tucked black dress that bespeak ladylike elegance and distance from the roughness of frontier life. All this is emphasized by her pretty gesture as she draws on a glove. The portrait, in all likelihood, was not painted in Minnesota but in St. Louis, where Mrs. Taliaferro had family connections and where she would travel occasionally for rather extended visits. It is possible that the picture is an early work of the Missouri artist George Caleb Bingham (1811–1879). The portrait bears enough resemblance to his early portraits (for instance that of James S. Rollins, 1834) to make such an attribution reasonable. There is the same hard drawing, the same treatment of mouth and chin, the same strong sculptural quality and feeling of immediate presence that makes the subject come alive. Moreover, the treatment of the landscape background indicates a groping toward the "layering" effect to suggest distance that Bingham achieved more successfully, though not differently, in his later work. Finally, a definite, though tenuous, family connection establishes a link between a Bingham subject and the Taliaferros.[11]

By the late 1830's and early 1840's Minnesota was attracting an increasing number of artists, both amateur and professional, for whom Fort Snelling was an important stop in the course of their western travels. One of these, John Mix Stanley (1814–1872), a native of Canandaigua, New York, was as fascinated by the West and its native inhabitants as Catlin had been. Also like Catlin, he had started his career as a portrait painter; but, after a year or two of portraying the citizens of Detroit and Chicago, he succumbed to the lure of western travel. He began his adventures at Fort Snelling in 1839, where he painted the local scene, and for the next fifteen years he traveled widely through the western territories. He was in the Minnesota Territory again fourteen years later when he joined Isaac Stevens's Pacific railroad survey. The Stevens expedition reached St. Paul on the evening of May 27, 1853, and stayed there for about a week while its planning

Fig. 5. Attributed to George C. Bingham. *Portrait of Mrs. Lawrence Taliaferro*. St. Paul. Courtesy of Minnesota Historical Society. Oil on canvas, 38 x 24 inches.

Fig. 6.
John Mix Stanley.
Prairie Indian Encampment.
Detroit. Courtesy of Detroit
Institute of Arts. Gift
of Mrs. Blanche F. Hooker.
Oil on canvas, 48⅛ x 36 inches.

and outfitting were completed. During that week Stanley was busy sketching. A drawing of St. Paul and one of Minnehaha Falls, or the "Laughing Waters," have survived as illustrations in the final report.[12]

While in Minnesota, Stanley had the help of an assistant artist named Max Strobel, about whom little is known. Strobel apparently abandoned the expedition soon after it left St. Paul, probably because Stevens, a notoriously driven man, insisted on a killing pace for both himself and his associates. Strobel, too, sketched views of St. Paul and other Minnesota scenes, and a contemporary reporter admired them enough to write of Strobel's "valuable service to Minnesota by his sketches of the Minnesota river from Lac qui Parle to Traverse des Sioux."[13]

Stanley, however, was made of sterner stuff and stayed with the Stevens expedition. He was determined to create a collection similar to Catlin's Indian Gallery. Unlike Catlin, Stanley developed his paintings in his eastern studio from the sketches he had made on his western travels. Much of his work, like Catlin's and Lewis's, was destroyed in the 1865 fire at the Smithsonian Institution, but enough remains to give a clear impression of his style. Moreover, much of his work was published in portfolio reproductions which found a ready market in the East and helped to popularize his image of what the West and its native inhabitants looked like. His *Prairie Indian Encampment* (fig. 6) may well have been painted in the Minnesota Territory and is typical of Stanley's early style. It is more deliberate, less spontaneous and free, than Catlin's Indian paintings, but on the other hand more carefully designed. His Indian tepees are solid, three-dimensional forms whose triangular contours add importance to the composition and provide an interesting contrast to the sprawling shapes of the Indians in the foreground. Though Stanley's later style is more consciously and deliberately monumental, his *Prairie Indian Encampment* is a direct and, one feels, accurate description of his visual experience in the West.

Fig. 7.
Charles Deas. *Indians at War.*
Omaha. Courtesy of Joslyn Museum of Art.
Collection of Northern Natural Gas Company.
Oil on canvas, 21 x 16⅞ inches.

Of all the artist-explorers of the 1840's, perhaps the best known among his own contemporaries was Charles Deas (1818–1867), who had nevertheless faded into oblivion by the end of the nineteenth century. Born in Philadelphia to a distinguished southern family, Deas, like Stanley, was inspired by Catlin's Indian Gallery and an exhibition he saw of it in 1838. After studying briefly at the National Academy of Design in New York and being elected an Associate National Academician in 1840 (a distinction not often bestowed on one of his age), Deas packed his gear and headed for Indian country. He stopped first at Fort Crawford, where his brother, George, was a young officer serving in the Fifth Infantry. In the following summer of 1841 he went up the Mississippi to Fort Snelling, where he painted the local scenic landmarks and portraits of the Sioux. He had some difficulties getting the Indians to pose, for they traditionally distrusted representational art. They feared that recognizable likenesses would "take away from their

bodies" or physically diminish them and eventually lead to their destruction. However, when one of their medicine men agreed to sit for his portrait, the others also overcame their reluctance and allowed Deas to "take their likenesses."

But Deas was interested in more than portraits. He eagerly depicted their dances, feasts, recitations, and the ball play for which the Sioux and the Chippewa were famous. He also painted Fort Snelling itself (plate 5). The picture is distinguished by a subtle manipulation of tone that serves to heighten the illusion of atmospheric perspective, and the standing figure of the Indian in the foreground serves to emphasize the setting of a frontier outpost. This painting is smaller and more intimate than most of Deas's works, and its delicacy of handling and soft color are in marked contrast to the larger, more dramatic pieces, such as *Indians at War* (fig. 7), which he painted later. The Fort Snelling view was probably painted as a personal memento of his visit to Minnesota, while the latter, a more imaginative work, was probably a studio piece, based on scenes he may have witnessed during his travels, but meant for popular consumption and distribution through the American Art Union. This important organization in American art history bought artists' works and distributed them through a lottery among its subscribers. Its importance in supporting American art and artists during its short life from 1839 to 1849 cannot be overemphasized; and Deas, as well as other important artists, was a regular contributor to it.

Probably in the same summer (1841) as the Fort Snelling view, Deas painted *Lion*, a large portrait of an Irish wolfhound belonging to Henry H. Sibley, Minnesota's territorial governor and later the first governor of the state.[14] Local tradition has it that Sibley owned as many as ten of these large dogs, whom he kept around the house before his marriage in 1843 to Sarah Jane Steele. That lady showed an understandable lack of enthusiasm for maintaining a large kennel in her home and insisted that the dogs establish residence in the carriage house. Lion, so the story goes, was so incensed at the loss of Sibley's favor to Sarah Jane that, in a fit of jealous rage, he jumped into the Minnesota River and swam across to Fort Snelling on the opposite shore. There he spent the rest of his years sulking over the fickle nature of man and the intransigence of woman.

Quite apart from the anecdotal nature of the painting, the portrait of Lion is important as a rare example of an American animal portrait, a genre popularized in England in the late eighteenth and early nineteenth century with portraits of the favorite horses of English country gentlemen. George Stubbs is the best known of this group of English animal painters, but there were others, too, whose pictures were widely known through the dissemination of the English sporting print. Deas could easily have been familiar with such sporting prints and, indeed, with the prints of other English artists as well, though this tie has yet to be properly investigated. It is particularly tempting to see a connection between Deas and Henry Fuseli, a Swiss-born English artist whose dramatic, even surrealist pictures of men and beasts might especially have influenced Deas's later pictures.[15]

In the fall of 1841 Deas headed south for St. Louis, where he set up a studio and acquired fame and a measure of financial success. He periodically returned to themes based on his Minnesota experience, however, with pictures, now lost, bearing such titles as *Sisseton Sioux Playing Ball*, *Interior of a Winnebago Lodge* and *Wenona*. It is possible that even the well-known *Voyageurs* (1847) was also inspired by the memory of his travels in the Minnesota Territory. After 1849, however, when he was committed to an asylum, suffering from "melancholia," Deas retreated increasingly to the world of imagination. His pictures became wilder and more fantastic though they continued to sell. He died in St. Louis in 1867 and was all too soon forgotten.

II Soldiers

In its early years, life in the Minnesota Territory was dominated by the military presence of Fort Snelling, the fort that was built in 1819 as the northernmost outpost in a chain of frontier garrisons established in 1817 by John C. Calhoun, secretary of war in the cabinet of President James Monroe. Fort Snelling's first commandant[1] was Colonel Josiah Snelling who oversaw the building of the fort and retained its command during the first difficult years of its existence. His task was aided by the presence of Lawrence Taliaferro, the young and very able Indian agent at the St. Peter's Agency, whose portrait has already been discussed. The likenesses of Colonel Snelling and his wife (figures 8, 9) by an anonymous portraitist, were painted in the East about 1818. Though the artist is unknown, he was obviously well trained in the fashionable neoclassic style of the period which favored monumental forms placed close to the picture plane, smooth, flowing lines, and clear, well-polished surfaces. Such portraits, when brought by their owners to the frontier communities, often served as the only models available to the local, self-taught artists struggling to create their own works of art with no formal instruction and few, if any, examples to guide them.

The artist most fully identified with Fort Snelling, and, indeed, with Minnesota in its early years is Seth Eastman (1808–1875), who is recognized today as one of the most important artists of the American West. Born in Maine in 1808, Eastman graduated in 1829 from West Point, where he had distinguished himself in its drawing classes. It should be no surprise that West Point was one of the best training grounds for artists in the nineteenth century, for before the perfection of the camera, sketching and drawing were recognized as important military skills, particularly at frontier outposts where the topography was unknown and the terrain uncharted. Eastman lost no time, therefore, on his first tours of duty at Fort Crawford in 1829 and at Fort Snelling in 1830 in sketching the land and the Indians nearby. The next two years were spent on reconnaissance work which took him on trips further west, after which he returned to West Point as assistant teacher of drawing. He resumed active duty in 1840 and, after a year in the Florida War, returned to Fort Snelling, serving there as a captain and commandant from 1841 to 1848. This time he brought his young family with him, two sons, a daughter, and his wife, Mary Henderson Eastman. Mary Eastman is important in her own right as the first person to collect and record in a comprehensive way the legends of the Sioux. She later published these in a number of books and articles on Indian themes, which her husband illustrated and which enjoyed a modest success in their own day.[2] Today they are regarded as quaint examples of nineteenth-century literature though they really deserve respectful attention as an early and rare effort to preserve the folklore of the Plains Indians.

When not occupied by his official duties at the post, Seth Eastman applied himself to recording visually the scenes around him. He was inventive enough to have been one of the first to use photographs as an aid in his finished paintings, employing an early type of daguerreotype camera to capture scenes of Indians dancing, reciting, playing games, and following their daily pursuits. He also used water colors, originally as a sketching tool, but later as an artistic medium in which he recognized an inherent aesthetic quality. Eastman was, in fact, the first American artist to do so, even before Winslow Homer, who is usually considered the pioneer of serious water-color artists.

The fact that Eastman later used these quick, spontaneous sketches in painting his more finished studio pieces does not diminish their own importance. They are, of course, interesting as historical documents of Plains Indian life, but they also reveal skillful draftsmanship, clear, fresh color, and a masterful ability to capture with a few sure strokes the image of a fleeting moment in a vanished world (fig. 10).

It is instructive to compare an Eastman water color with an oil painting based on it, for this reveals an important aspect of the nineteenth-century white man's image of the Indian. The tendency of many western artists, Eastman and Catlin among them, was to regard the Indian as both Rousseau's "noble savage" and an exemplar of the virtues associated with the heroes of classical antiquity. This attitude was part of the neoclassic revival of the nineteenth century, whose iconography is a curious blend of sentimentality and primitivism in nature, emphasizing such "antique" virtues as fortitude, a civic sense, and skill at oratory. Such virtues are often implicitly attributed to the Indians in Eastman's finished oil paintings by

Fig. 8. Anon. *Colonel Josiah Snelling*, c. 1818. St. Paul. Courtesy of Minnesota Historical Society. Oil on canvas, 28 x 23 inches.

Fig. 9. Anon. *Mrs. Josiah Snelling*, c. 1818. St. Paul. Courtesy of Minnesota Historical Society. Oil on canvas, 30 x 24 inches.

Fig. 10. Seth Eastman. *Guarding the Cornfields*, 1850. St. Paul. Courtesy of James
Jerome Hill Reference Library. Water color, 19½ x 13⅛ inches.

transforming a sketch of a Sioux, an Ojibway, or a Winnebago into a copy of a classical statue.

Compare, for example, the water-color sketch *The Death Whoop* (fig. 11) with the oil painting of the same subject (fig. 12). The most easily distinguished difference lies in the details of clothing. The fallen victim in the water color wears a patterned shirt of cheap cotton, and the triumphant warrior holding a scalp above him is dressed in a patched and tattered garment that can best be described as nondescript. In the oil version both victim and victor are dressed with greater dignity and care. The former now wears a white shirt with the full folds that suggest the drapery on classical sculpture. The triumphant Indian holds a bow as well as a scalp in his hand, the bow, of course, connoting a more noble weapon than the scalping knife and also one more appropriate to classical heroes. His pose now conforms, more obviously than in the sketch, to such classical prototypes as, for example, the Apollo Belvedere. Plaster casts of this Apollo were standard models in the art classes of the nineteenth century, including those at West Point. Even the dead man is less lumpishly portrayed, a touch of grace having been given the fallen victim. The group suggests in spirit, if not in detail, the late Hellenistic statue of a Gaulish chieftain slaying his wife before killing himself to avoid facing death at the hands of the enemy. As the ancient sculptor admired the barbarian Gauls in the moment of their heroic death, so, too, did Seth Eastman romanticize the noble savage who, in the wild, free life of the uncivilized West, asked for no mercy and gave none.

Finally, one might note that even the landscape setting is transformed in the studio piece. The suggestion of barren hills and untidy scrub has now become the deep and luminous landscape of Eastman's best work. The distant hills reflect a rosy glow, and the soft light creates a sense of peace that mitigates the violence of the pictured scene.

The same sense of atmosphere and far horizons is to be found in a fine, though little known, Eastman painting entitled *Indian on the Lookout* (plate 6).

Fig. 11. Seth Eastman. *The Death Whoop.* St. Paul.
Courtesy of James Jerome Hill Reference Library.
Water color, 12½ x 9½ inches.

Fig. 12. Seth Eastman. *The Death Whoop.* Washington,
D.C. Courtesy of Architect of the Capitol.
Oil on canvas, 38½ x 28 inches.

Here a solitary Indian, seated on a low outcropping of rock, faces away from us to gaze at a vast, river-fed valley far below. The landscape is a particularly beautiful one, evoking a sense of space, clear light, and tranquil countryside. Although it bears some resemblance to southeastern Minnesota, it is also similar to the landscapes of the Hudson River School of American painting, to which Eastman, in fact, belongs.[3] West Point, where he studied, is, of course, located on the Hudson River near the Catskill Mountain highlands and is therefore at the very center of the area favored by the first generation of Hudson River artists. Their reverence for nature and specifically for the American wilderness led them to sketch and paint nature directly and out-of-doors. In this respect they were the first "plein air" painters of the nineteenth century. The sense of man at one with nature is a further link between Eastman's painting and the Hudson River School. The unity of man and nature is not always peaceful, however. Thus, in *Indian on the Lookout* the bow as well as the Indian's watchful attitude suggests potential violence. Similarly, the dead branches on the hillside that have been twisted by some long-vanished storm show that nature as well as man occasionally erupts with malevolent and destructive power.

Another painter associated with Fort Snelling in its early days is Sergeant Edward K. Thomas (1817–1906), whose *View of Fort Snelling* (plate 7) was erroneously attributed to Seth Eastman for many years.[4] Thomas was stationed at the fort from 1849 to 1851 and while there painted a number of views of the fort which he produced almost as souvenirs of the frontier outpost.[5] He was a more primitive painter than Eastman and probably self-taught. Though he was born in Philadelphia, a center for art studies in the early nineteenth century, and even did some portrait painting there, he is not known to have attended any art school either there or elsewhere. He made the army his career and only after his retirement in 1865 did he turn to painting as a full-time occupation. The Detroit city directories list him, from 1878 to 1898, as "painter," "artist," and once "fresco and ornamental painter,"

but only one painting, a self-portrait, survives from this long period. He died in Detroit in 1906 at the age of eighty-nine.

Several characteristics in Thomas's *View of Fort Snelling* betray the hand of an unsophisticated artist. Unlike the single vantage point perspective used by Seth Eastman, for example, Sergeant Thomas's landscape stretches out, maplike, before us. Such a bird's-eye view is typical of the primitive artist who tends to scatter precisely detailed objects throughout the scene with little regard for compositional unity or the blurring of distant forms in the haze of atmosphere. Thus, the fort in the background is as clearly defined as the Indian tepees in the foreground, and Pike's Island merely occupies space on the canvas without convincingly receding into the distance. A profusion of decorative detail and a rather harsh color scheme also serve to identify Thomas's work and separate it from Eastman's.

During the period of Seth Eastman's command at Fort Snelling, a young artist, Swiss born and Paris trained, appeared there briefly, though long enough to leave his own impression of the fort. John Caspar Wild (c. 1806–1846), who painted the view of Fort Snelling in plate 8, had settled first in Philadelphia upon his arrival in America but in 1835 moved to Cincinnati. He worked there for three years as a landscape painter and lithographer before moving back to Philadelphia in 1838. The following year he succumbed to the lure of the West and settled in St. Louis, where he conceived the idea of painting a series of frontier forts. Though all of these are finished paintings, it is possible that they were studies for a large-scale panorama that Wild never actually completed. In any event, he is known to have been in Fort Snelling in 1844. His representation of the fort is much more academically accomplished than Sergeant Thomas's and is similar, in fact, to Seth Eastman's view which hangs today in the United States Capitol. Wild's picture, in water color and gouache, is essentially a picturesque and idealized view, soft in tone though precisely drawn. It is, in fact, a fitting illustration of a contemporary literary description of

Fig. 13. Alfred Sully. *Upper Sioux Agency, Valley of the Minnesota.* New Haven. Courtesy of The Beinecke Rare Book and Manuscript Library, Yale University. Water color, 3¾ x 4¾ inches.

the fort. "The scenery around Fort Snelling, which is situated on a high limestone bluff . . . is of a sublime and impressive character. Huge slabs of rock in the bed of the river and the towering cliffs on either side, reveal the existence of a mighty cataract in a remote age of the world, of which the receding Falls of St. Anthony now present only the diminshed remains."[6] Wild disappeared from the scene as abruptly as he had appeared. In 1845 he was living in Davenport, Iowa, where he died the following year.

Though Wild was not, as far as is known, a soldier or even a military expeditioner, his association with Fort Snelling in its early days suggests his inclusion in this chapter. A direct connection with the military characterizes General Alfred Sully (1820–1879), however, who in 1863 led an expedition against the Sioux in Minnesota.[7] Alfred Sully was a son of Thomas Sully, Philadelphia's most sought-after portrait painter during the first half of the nineteenth century. The son apparently preferred the sword to the pen (or brush), even though he had considerable skill with the latter. On an earlier trip to Minnesota, he had sketched the Upper Sioux Agency (fig. 13). During the summer of 1856, the then Captain Sully accompanied Company K of the Second Infantry under the command of Major George Washington Patten from Fort Ripley in the Minnesota Territory to Fort Pierre in the Dakota Territory. Patten later wrote a lively account of the march under the title "Over the Prairie," the unpublished manuscript of which is in Yale University's Collection of Manuscripts of Western Americana.[8] The narrative describes with humor and a feeling for colorful detail the incidents of army life on the prairies and in the frontier outposts. The account was made even more vivid by the twenty-one drawings and water colors that were executed by Captain Sully

Fig. 14. Alfred Sully. *Ft. Snelling*, 1856. New Haven. Courtesy of The Beinecke
Rare Book and Manuscript Library, Yale University. Water color, 3¾ x 6⅓ inches.

to accompany it. Four of these were of Minnesota sites, including one of Fort Snelling (fig. 14). They are further evidence of the importance of eyewitness sketches to the growing knowledge of what frontier America looked like.

More that pertains to the history of art in early Minnesota survives in the work of Frank Blackwell Mayer (1827–1899). Although he was not a soldier himself, he attached himself to the military and came to Minnesota in the summer of 1851 to witness the signing of the Treaty of Traverse des Sioux. President Fillmore had appointed Alexander Ramsey, then governor of the Minnesota Territory, and Luke Lea, United States commissioner of Indian affairs, to make a treaty with the Indians, which ceded to the white man an estimated thirty-five million acres in what is now southern Minnesota, Iowa, and South Dakota. Mayer, a young Baltimore artist, realized that the gathering of the Sioux nations by the thousands in the Minnesota Valley to participate in the treaty negotiations would be a colorful event, picturesque enough for the most demanding painter's brush. Moreover, Mayer felt that "in his choice of subjects . . . an artist should select those peculiarly illustrative of the history of his own country."[9] The artist had, in fact, attempted to obtain an appointment in Washington as official artist to the expedition, and, though he failed in this, he did meet Seth Eastman (then living in Washington) who gave the young man encouragement, advice, and useful letters of introduction.

So Mayer turned his steps westward without official blessing but, as he wrote in his journal, "determined to undertake the trip at my own expense as the intercourse with the Indians and others and the sketches I shall make will amply repay me for any expenditure I shall make."[10] Mayer was well equipped

*Sketched in the lodge of "Rda-ma-nee"
[the walking rattler] at ~~Traverse des Sioux~~
["the village in the corner"]*

Nancy McLure.
Winona.
July 4th 1851. Traverse des Sioux.

Fig. 15. Frank Blackwell Mayer. *Nancy McLure*, 1851.
Chicago. Courtesy of Newberry Library. Ayer
Collection. Drawing, 4 x 7 inches.

for undertaking this sort of trip, for he had studied art under a Baltimore artist of exceptional talent, Alfred Jacob Miller (1810–1874).[11] Miller himself had traveled as far west as the Rocky Mountains in 1837 as a member of an expedition led by a Scottish adventurer, Sir William Drummond Stewart. Some years later, Miller painted a series of large pictures for Murthly Castle, Stewart's ancestral home in Perthshire, Scotland, based on sketches he had made during their western travels. It is possible that Miller's tales of his adventures in the West stimulated Mayer's desire to join a western expedition himself.

In any event, Mayer left Baltimore in May, 1851, and journeyed by railroad, stagecoach, and steamboat to the Minnesota Territory. On June 29 he joined the commissioners for the trip to Traverse des Sioux, a rude trading post and mission station near present-day St. Peter, Minnesota. Here he had ample opportunity to observe and sketch the thousands of Indians gathered there and to describe his impressions of them in sketches and in journal entries. Both these sources vividly re-create pioneer Minnesota with its white settlers, Indian people, men and women of mixed blood (fig. 15),[12] the dragoons at Fort Snelling, the traders and voyageurs from the Canadian settlements, the carts, the keelboats, the tepees and cabins, and, above all, the camp at the treaty site of Traverse des Sioux (fig. 16). These unpretentious sketches, perhaps because of their very informality, provide a clear and graphic picture of Minnesota's history in the making a century and a quarter ago.

Much later in his life, after a period of extended European travel and some study in the Paris ateliers of Charles Gleyre and Gustave Brion and when the artist had settled permanently in the city of Annapolis, Maryland, he tried to interest the Minnesota legislature in a large oil painting based on his sketches of the Treaty of Traverse des Sioux. The project went as far as a large oil sketch which he sent to Minnesota in 1885. There the project ended, for, much to the artist's disappointment, funds for the finished work were not forthcoming. In 1903, however, four years after Mayer's death, interest in the painting was revived when commissions for paintings and murals for

Fig. 16. Frank Blackwell Mayer. *Treaty Site of Traverse des Sioux*, 1851. Chicago. Courtesy of Newberry Library. Ayer Collection. Pencil drawing, 10 x 13 inches.

the new State Capitol were assigned. Cass Gilbert, the architect of the Capitol, commissioned Francis D. Millet to paint a picture of the Treaty of Traverse des Sioux and instructed him to "follow a sketch which was made by Mr. Mayer . . . who was present at the time."[13] Millet's picture based on Mayer's sketch, though differing somewhat from the original compo-

sition, now hangs in a place of honor in the governor's reception room in the Capitol. Perhaps because of its formality, however, and the constraints under which it was produced, it fails to capture the tangible sense of being present at the scene that is apparent in the sketches drawn by the youthful adventurer in pioneer Minnesota half a century before.

III Painters of the Panorama

In the middle of the nineteenth century, a new enthusiasm seized a number of American artists who thought they had discovered a potential source of undreamed-of riches for themselves. This was the painted panorama which sought to capture on large-scale canvases historic scenes or spectacular landscape views. It was a form of painting that had enjoyed some success as a popular entertainment in the capitals of Europe and there had attracted the notice of a few American artists. Robert Fulton had painted a panorama in Paris and supported himself by its proceeds while working on the inventions for which he later became famous (including, incidentally, the steamboat, which had a unique importance in the settlement of the western territories). John Vanderlyn did several panoramas. He spent a fortune building a rotunda in New York to display a very large one he had painted of Versailles.[1] Vanderlyn's panoramas were cumbersome, however, and static in effect, when what was wanted was the nineteenth-century equivalent of Cinerama. Thus, in the 1830's a new kind of panorama appeared which was less a portable mural than, literally, a moving picture. This consisted of a large strip of canvas which was unwound, section by section, from two vertical rollers. Often there was accompanying music, commentary on the unfolding scenes, and even juggling and acrobatic acts to attract the public and their admission fees.

The panorama painters became especially attracted, in the 1830's and 1840's, to the Mississippi River Valley, whose broad sweep and expansive views lent themselves well to this form of popular amusement. The panorama was, in fact, a form of theater, employing the broad, quick style of the scene painter and often tricks of showmanship such as the real smoke and steam that poured from the model steamboats pulled in front of one panorama of the Mississippi done by Leon D. Pomarede.

Pomarede (c. 1807–1892) was a French landscapist and mural painter who arrived in New Orleans in 1830. Though he had probably already had some artistic training in Europe, he received further instruction in New Orleans from two theatrical scene painters before moving up the river to St. Louis in 1832. He was associated briefly in 1848 with Henry Lewis in a panorama project, but the association did not last long. In the spring of 1849 he journeyed upriver to the Falls of St. Anthony with a young St. Louis assistant named Carl Wimar (1828–1862), who was later to make an important name for himself as a painter of the American West. Pomarede's idea was to create a giant panorama of the Mississippi River from its headwaters of navigation to its confluence with the Ohio River. Sixty-five feet of the work which he eventually produced, *Panorama of the Mississippi River and Indian Life*, were devoted to a representation of Brown's

Falls—later Minnehaha Falls—and a Winnebago encampment on the neighboring prairie. Though perhaps not the most artistically sophisticated of this genre, it was certainly the most entertaining, for it boasted a buffalo hunt, a prairie fire, an Indian war dance, mechanical, moving steamboats, and a "view of the Great Fire of St. Louis, on the night of the 17th May, representing that awful and terrific conflagration in all its fury, as it appeared to the distracted citizens." It was a huge commercial success from its first showing in St. Louis in 1849 to its unfortunate destruction by fire in Newark, New Jersey, in 1850. Discouraged by its loss, Pomarede returned to St. Louis, abandoned panorama painting, and occupied himself for the rest of his life with religious and genre pictures and murals for churches, theaters, and public buildings.

Another lost panorama of the Mississippi of even more ambitious scope was the "Three Mile Painting" begun by John Banvard (1815–1891) in 1840. But though the work that was his proudest achievement has disappeared, we know, through his self-portrait (fig. 17), what the artist-showman looked like. Banvard was born and brought up in New York City, but he left home at fifteen and went west to Louisville, Kentucky, which in 1830 was still pretty much of a frontier town. He worked for a short time in a store there before becoming an itinerant portraitist. During the later 1830's he worked along the Ohio and Mississippi rivers, gradually conceiving the plan of painting an enormous panorama of the Mississippi.[2] He began work on it in 1840 and finished it in the autumn of 1846. It was billed as *Banvard's Panorama of the Mississippi and Missouri Rivers, Painted on Three Miles of Canvas, Exhibiting a View of the Country 3,000 Miles in Length, Extending from the Mouth of the Yellowstone River to the City of New Orleans, Being by Far the Largest Picture Ever Executed by Man.*

To gather material for "the largest picture ever executed by man," Banvard spent a year traveling along the Mississippi River, making drawings and sketches which were later transferred to a large roll of canvas in his Louisville studio. When it was completed he took it to Boston and New York, and then to Paris and

Fig. 17. John Banvard. *Self-Portrait.* St. Paul.
Courtesy of Minnesota Historical Society.
Oil on canvas, 30 x 25 inches.

London, where it was presented to Queen Victoria at Windsor Castle. The success of his spectacle encouraged the artist to undertake other projects of similar magnificence, including one of the Nile River later displayed in a museum of Egyptian artifacts in London. Eventually Banvard returned to the United States and in 1880 he moved with his family to Watertown, South Dakota, where he settled down to painting pictures on a more modest scale and to writing poetry, plays, novels, and travel books.

Melodrama, in painting no less than on the stage, seems to have been the temper of the times and "panorama fever" raged on. John Mix Stanley succumbed to it as did others less well known. John Rowson Smith (1810–1864) painted what he called a "Leviathan of a Panorama of the Mississippi River," which he exhibited successfully to an enthusiastic public. So did Samuel B. Stockwell (1813–1854), who was an actor and scene painter in Boston's Tremont Theater before coming to St. Louis in the 1840's where he worked with Henry Lewis on a Mississippi panorama. Then there was John J. Egan (active 1850–1851), an Irish painter who produced a diorama in motion of the Mississippi based on sketches by Dr. Montrouth W. Dickeson, a Philadelphia physician and amateur archaeologist. Even Seth Eastman contemplated painting a Mississippi panorama, for between 1846 and 1848 he produced a portfolio of small water colors portraying the river from the Falls of St. Anthony to below the mouth of the Ohio River. Although he included Indian figures in many of them, it is the river itself that is the real subject of these paintings, with the precise location of each scene carefully identified by the artist in preparation, apparently, for a much larger project.

Though Eastman never carried out such a project, his friend Henry Lewis did. Lewis (1819–1904) owned a number of Eastman water-color sketches, and the panorama he eventually produced had at least seventeen scenes based on Eastman originals.[3] When Lewis first thought of a panorama project, he was living in St. Louis and, like so many panorama painters, was engaged in theater-related work. He was, in fact, a stage carpenter in a St. Louis opera house, an occupation which apparently proved too small for his ambitions. Lewis's background was typical of the frontier artist. He had been born in England and was living in Boston when he was seized with a thirst for adventure and set out for the West. In 1836 he settled in St. Louis where, though entirely self-taught, he took up art as a profession. At different times he was associated, briefly, with Leon Pomarede and Samuel Stockwell in their panorama projects, but his relationship with them was far from tranquil. Eventually, all three created their own panoramas, all of which had been exhibited in St. Louis by 1849.

Henry Lewis's panorama, now lost, led a fascinating and checkered career of its own, ending up eventually as a treasured curiosity in the possession of a Javanese prince.[4] Perhaps some day it will turn up in the jungles of Southeast Asia, but if it does not, we have, nevertheless, a fairly good idea of what it looked like. In the first place, there still exist a number of oil paintings by the artist that were based on sketches for the project. There also survives a journal Lewis kept of a canoe voyage he took in 1848 from the Falls of St. Anthony to St. Louis. Most important of all, however, many scenes that were based on the panorama were later published in a book he wrote about the Mississippi River Valley while he was living far away from it. *Das Illustrierte Mississippithal* was published in German in 1858 in the city of Düsseldorf, where Lewis went after touring America and Europe with his panorama.[5] His choice was a natural one, for Düsseldorf was, in the nineteenth century, a center for both publishing and art. The Düsseldorf Academy was, indeed, an important influence in American painting, because, from the 1840's on, it attracted a large number of American art students. It stressed a dry, meticulous, and rather theatrical landscape style which fit in well with the literalness of much of the art of the period. In any event, Lewis found its atmosphere congenial. He settled in Düsseldorf in 1853, after having enrolled in the academy to fill the gaps in his artistic education. In 1867 he applied for the post of American consular agent there, to which he was duly appointed and in which he served until 1884. Although he maintained a deep interest in America and retained his family ties there, he returned only once, in the 1880's, to attend a family wedding in St. Louis. He died in Germany in 1904 at the age of eighty-five.

Though Lewis's panorama has disappeared and the Mississippi scenes in his book survive only in published lithographs, his technique and style can still be judged from several extant paintings. One of these, *The Gorge of the St. Croix* (plate 9), is typical of Lewis's technique before he went to Düsseldorf. It is a clear, direct, and literal description of the scene, showing the steamer *Cora* discharging passengers at a narrow wooden boathouse tucked into a cleft of the rocky shore. Another view on the same scenic river, *Cheever's Mill on the St. Croix*, can be seen in both an oil sketch on paper (fig. 18) and a finished oil painting based on it (fig. 19). The sketch is a quick impression of the scene that captures a strong feeling of time and space and evokes an immediate recognition of the artist's experience. It vividly suggests a rushing stream, pine-covered palisades, and rough wooden buildings in a wilderness clearing. All these are transformed in the later picture into something neater, tighter, and more consciously pictorial. The splash of white water is now a tidy waterfall sending waves of careful ripples down the river. The woodland clearing has become a little settlement inhabited by industrious workmen and visited by neighboring Indians. The dugout canoe being steered purposefully toward shore now contains three carefully defined boatmen, and even the logs on the shore are no longer flung carelessly about but are laid out in orderly rows ready for the sawmill's blades. It is obviously a carefully finished picture. The houses, people, and landscape elements are shown with a kind of hard linearity and precise detailing that defines distant objects as clearly as near ones. In spite of the bright colors and the soft light that casts the scene in a rosy glow, the general effect is of a "posed" landscape rather than a spontaneous expression of the artist's own experience.

A later picture by Lewis of a Minnesota scene, *St. Anthony Falls* (plate 10), was actually painted while the artist was living in Germany. Signed and dated 1855, it was based on sketches made in 1848 for the panorama, but it reflects the dry, tight style of the Düsseldorf landscape tradition. Though the scene recedes more convincingly into the distance than the earlier pictures and the softening effect of atmosphere is better understood, it is obviously a studio piece meant to evoke the spirit of adventure in far places. The Indian, who is sitting on a rocky ledge in the foreground, puffing on his long-stemmed pipe, serves to indicate scale and also to define the location of the scene in a remote outpost of civilization. Here nature's nobleman still lives in simple harmony with his surroundings, and though dark clouds rise to threaten the sunny landscape, the unspoken and perhaps half-conscious message is that the pretenses of civilized life have not yet corrupted this American Eden.

One final panorama deserves mention in this chapter and fortunately, it is still extant. This is the one painted by John Stevens (1816–1879) of Rochester describing both the dangers and the rewards of life in the Minnesota Territory. Much, though not all of it, was devoted to a rather bloody representation of the Indian war of 1862, a subject that captured the public imagination and retained its popular appeal long after the events themselves had become a part of one of the darker chapters in our national history.

John Stevens was a self-taught artist who earned his living as a sign, wagon, and house painter. Born in western New York State, he moved successively to Illinois, Wisconsin, and finally southern Minnesota, where he settled in 1853. There he built a farmhouse and a makeshift studio on a plot of ground that later became the center of Rochester. Perhaps in Rochester, which became an entertainment center for the area, Stevens first saw one of the Mississippi panoramas that were so popular in the mid-nineteenth century and conceived the idea of using that vehicle for a representation of the Sioux massacre. Panoramas of the "Father of Waters" would, he felt sure, seem tame by comparison, and the sensational nature of his own "moving picture," emphasized by a "liberal use of red paint," would assure it commercial success.

Fig. 18. Henry Lewis. *Cheever's Mill on the St. Croix*, 1848. St. Paul. Courtesy of
Minnesota Historical Society. Oil sketch, 8 11/16 x 11 3/16 inches.

Fig. 19. Henry Lewis. *Cheever's Mill on the St. Croix*. Minneapolis. Courtesy of The Minneapolis Institute of Arts. The Julia B. Bigelow Fund. Oil on canvas, 20 x 30 inches.

Fig. 20. John Stevens. *Minnesota Fruit*. Detail from panorama, 1872. St. Paul.
Courtesy of Minnesota Historical Society. Panel #26. 6 x 7 feet.

Stevens did not depend on gore alone to make his panorama popular. He was too good a showman for that. Interspersed among the bloodier scenes were some of a more peaceful nature, providing relief from unmitigated horror. There were such items of current interest as a balloon ascension in Brooklyn and the Great Chicago Fire. Washington welcoming Lafayette and his family was also, rather incongruously, included and, best of all, a delightful scene called *Minnesota Fruit* (fig. 20). In this panel a tree is shown in full bloom, bearing children rather than the more usual product. Three women beneath the tree prepare to catch the falling infants as they drop like ripe peaches from the tree. When it was first displayed in Roches-

ter in 1873, it "attracted much attention and drew forth loud applause."[6] We can easily understand why.

Stevens actually painted several Sioux massacre panoramas, the first one in 1862, right after the event itself, and later versions in 1868, 1870, and 1872. Billed as "Stevens's Great Tableau Paintings Representing the Indian Massacre of 1862," the first panorama was shown at La Crosse, Wisconsin, and St. Paul, Minnesota, in 1862. It was accompanied by a running commentary delivered by one Captain C. E. Sencerbox, who was identified as "one of the oldest and most popular steamboatmen of the upper river."[7] Other tricks of showmanship included a traveling sleigh with "sides of transparent canvas on which [were]

Fig. 21. John Stevens. *Flight from the Sioux Uprising*. Detail from panorama, 1872.
St. Paul. Courtesy of Minnesota Historical Society. Panel #7. 6 x 7 feet.

painted striking advertisements of the show" and which were lit at night from inside the vehicle, where a portable stove kept the exhibitors snug and warm in the Minnesota winter. For a while "Professor Earl, the Great Violinist and Songster," provided musical accompaniment, and in a less cheerful vein a young survivor of the massacre appeared in person to comment on the scenes as they were unrolled before the public.

Painted in the crude, primitive style of the untutored artist, the Stevens panorama depends on the details of the continuous narrative to achieve its dramatic effect (fig. 21). There is little attempt at representing the illusion of space, for the figures and ob-

jects are crowded into the scene with little regard for linear or atmospheric perspective. Similarly, there is little attempt at modeling or at suggesting the contrast of light and shadow that defines forms in real space. It is the narrative itself that describes the action rather than the figures in it. In spite of its awkwardness, however, and its many faults of composition, perspective, and human anatomy, the pictures have a refreshing earnestness that endows them with a value of their own. If they are naive, they are also direct and, pictorially at least, unpretentious. Above all, they provided entertainment of a particularly graphic kind for the unsophisticated audiences of Minnesota's frontier villages and towns.

IV Tourists and Travelers

By the 1850's, the decade of its admission to the Union, Minnesota was fast becoming settled territory. Homesteads were staked out, crops planted, industries started, and towns and cities founded. Most important of all, however, for its ties with the rest of the world, a regular steamboat schedule started operating in 1847, instead of the sporadic arrivals and departures—depending on cargo—that had previously been in effect. In the 1860's railroads, too, began to provide regular service to the new state of Minnesota, cementing even more closely its ties to the settled East.

It was still very much of a frontier area, of course—rough, crude, and unfailingly optimistic about its future. But if, with increasing settlement, it began to lose something of the romance associated with the wild, uncivilized West, it nevertheless still boasted many areas of unspoiled natural beauty picturesque enough to attract the more adventurous tourists from the East.

The main attraction was the great river itself, touted as a sightseer's paradise as early as 1835 by none other than George Catlin. He described his trip up the "majestic river . . . from the mouth of the Ouisconsin to the Falls of St. Anthony" as having filled his "high-wrought mind" with "amazement and wonder." He then proposed a "Fashionable Tour," a trip by steamer to Rock Island, Galena, Dubuque, Prairie du Chien, Lake Pepin, St. Peter's, and the Falls of St. Anthony, pointing out that it was the only part of the great "'Far West' . . . to which *ladies* can have access."[1] The idea of a fashionable tour up the Mississippi quickly spread, and artists, among others, booked passage on the steamboats. These tourists, in search of fresh and novel subjects for their brush, were also well aware of the presence of Indians, those "noble savages" of the West, who would lend just the right note of the "picturesque" to their paintings of the far frontier. And though a few of these artist-tourists were men of established reputations, most were young adventurers on the thresholds of their careers, embarking on a western trip before settling down to the more serious business of life in the studios of Boston, New York, and Philadelphia.

Another probable stimulus to the Mississippi tour was the popularity of Longfellow's poem *The Song of Hiawatha*, published in 1854. This poem, whose setting was the lakes and forests of the Minnesota Territory, was the first in American literature to recognize Indian legends as powerful themes for imaginative writing. Furthermore, the source of Longfellow's inspiration is worth noting. *The Song of Hiawatha* was based on Henry Schoolcraft's book on the Indians, a debt the poet was careful to acknowledge. But Schoolcraft's work itself depended, for much of its information on Indian lore, on the writings of Mary Henderson Eastman, who had gathered her material while living in the Minnesota Territory.[2] And, as we have already noted, both Mrs. Eastman's work and Schoolcraft's enjoyed the added advantage of illustrations by Seth Eastman, commandant from 1841 to 1848 of the frontier outpost of Fort Snelling.

Among the artists visiting Minnesota in the 1850's was Eastman Johnson (1824–1906), a native of Lowell, Maine. He began his artistic career in Boston in the mid-1840's painting crayon portraits of his friends and neighbors. They included, as an influential patron, Henry Wadsworth Longfellow himself. Drawn, like many other mid-century students, to the Royal Academy of Art at Düsseldorf, Johnson studied there from 1849 to 1851 under the tutelage of both German professors and the American artist Emanuel Leutze. From there he went to Holland, where he carefully studied Rembrandt and other Dutch masters and where he was so highly thought of that, according to one source, he was even offered the position of court painter.[3] He declined the honor, however, and went on to Paris, where he entered the studio of the French academic painter Thomas Couture, from which he was abruptly called home by the death of his mother in 1855. By then, however, he had acquired the rudiments of an eclectic European education and had absorbed it into his own personal style.

Johnson's interest for us lies in the fact that in 1856 and for a longer period in 1857 he visited and painted in the Superior-Duluth area. His sister, Sarah, was married to William H. Newton of Superior, and his brother, Reuben, owned a sawmill there. He visited them briefly in the summer of 1856 and, sitting on the porch of his sister's house, painted a casual view of Duluth and a view across the lake, *Minnesota Point* (plate 11). He returned the next summer for a longer stay, for he had become fascinated by the Chippewa Indians and wanted to sketch them in their natural setting. Johnson traveled 150 miles to one of their camps at Grand Portage and stayed through the following winter, completing fifteen oil paintings and twenty charcoal drawings. The collection he left is

a unique pictorial record of the Chippewa in the Duluth area almost a century and a quarter ago.

The painting *Grand Portage* (fig. 22) is an early example of Johnson's ability to manipulate light and shadow to suggest form, a technique he may well have learned from his study of Rembrandt and other Dutch masters. It was a technique that he had not used in his 1856 picture of Duluth and that, for some reason, he later abandoned, returning to it after many years in a series of paintings of cranberry pickers on Nantucket Island. In the later examples the slanting light defines even more vividly than in the earlier ones the shapes of the human figures, but the sharp light-and-shadow style makes its first tentative appearance in the artist's early Minnesota scenes.

Though the Grand Portage landscapes are presented with little visual editorializing—merely as impressions of everyday life among the Chippewa— the pastel portrait *Hiawatha* (plate 12) is both a more finished work and a more romantic one. It portrays the Indian sitting in a woodland glade, facing away from the observer and absorbed in his own quiet thoughts. This is the closest Johnson came to expressing the idea of the noble savage, especially as it embodies Rousseau's idea of the innocent and virtuous child of nature. The brightly colored costume, which still exists,[4] enriches the picture but in no way detracts from its mood of silent contemplation.

Other paintings of Eastman Johnson's sojourn among the Chippewa portray them sitting, walking, riding in canoes, or standing beside their tepees. There is a particularly fine series of portraits (figs. 23, 24, and 25), some of which are drawings in crayon and charcoal. They are striking studies of a proud and dignified people, drawn with the sensitive and unerring line of the master draftsman. Johnson felt a particular attachment to these drawings and paintings, for he refused to sell them, and though he occasionally showed them to friends, they were never exhibited during his lifetime.[5]

For Johnson, and for other touring artists too, a trip up the Mississippi River to the Minnesota Territory was a youthful adventure, a trip to a far frontier whose

Fig. 22. Eastman Johnson. *Grand Portage*, 1857. Duluth. Courtesy of St. Louis County
Historical Society. Oil on canvas, 7¾ x 13 inches.

Fig. 23. Eastman Johnson. *Double Head Study: Indians*, 1857. Duluth. Courtesy of
St. Louis County Historical Society. Oil on canvas, 7 x 11½ inches.

Fig. 25. Eastman Johnson. *Kennewawbemit*, 1857. Duluth.
Courtesy of St. Louis County Historical Society.
Charcoal, 8 x 7½ inches.

Fig. 24.
Eastman Johnson. *Medosuabeek*, 1857. Duluth.
Courtesy of St. Louis County Historical Society.
Charcoal, 20½ x 10½ inches.

Fig. 26. George F. Fuller. *Maiden Rock, Lake Pepin*, 1853. St. Paul. Courtesy of
Minnesota Historical Society. Water color, 3¼ x 6 inches.

memory they would treasure in later life. Among those who enjoyed such a summer adventure was George F. Fuller (1822–1884), a farmer from Deerfield, Massachusetts, who is well known in American art as a painter of brooding figures inhabiting a hazy world of twilight and shadow. In the summer of 1853 Fuller apparently traveled up the Mississippi River, painting and sketching the scenic spots along the way. His water color of Maiden Rock, Lake Pepin (fig. 26), and his sketches of Fort Snelling and Minnehaha Falls, are more precise and linear in style than his later dreamier and more poetic pictures. They are evidence of the work of a young, mostly self-taught artist before his exposure to the great examples of European art which were to strongly influence his later work.[6]

Another artist who visited the Minnesota Territory in the 1850's was a German-American of obscure reputation whose talents—both as pictorial historian and as accomplished draftsman—deserve more recognition than they have yet received. Adolf Johann Hoeffler (1825–1898) was born in Frankfurt, Germany, the son of a painter from whom he received his first les-

sons in art. After further study in the Düsseldorf Academy, he left for America, arriving in New Orleans in 1848, and spent the next years as an itinerant artist, painting portraits for a living and filling his sketchbooks with drawings of the landscapes he saw on his travels. He went up the Mississippi by steamboat, reaching St. Paul in the summer of 1849. There he painted portraits of Mrs. Alexander Ramsey and her child, for which the territorial governor paid him fifty dollars.[7] Half a dozen sketches of Fort Snelling and other landmarks survive from this trip. The artist appeared in the territory again in the fall of 1852, when he sketched more Minnesota scenes in preparation for an article entitled "Sketches of the Upper Mississippi" that was published in *Harper's New Monthly Magazine* in July, 1853. With the article appeared seventeen woodcuts based on the artist's drawings. One of these is a pencil sketch, *St. Paul* in 1852 (fig. 27), while another illustrates on one sheet a double view, *Lake Harriet and Lake of the Isles* (fig. 28). They afford a fascinating glimpse of these well-loved Minneapolis lakes as they appeared a century and a

Fig. 27. Adolf Hoeffler. *St. Paul, Minnesota Territory*, 1852. St. Paul. Courtesy of Minnesota Historical Society. Pencil sketch, 12 x 18½ inches.

Fig. 28. Adolf Hoeffler. *Lake Harriet and Lake of the Isles*, 1852. St. Paul. Courtesy of Minnesota Historical Society. Pencil sketch, 13 x 20 inches.

quarter ago. Hoeffler also sketched a more finished picture of Minnehaha Falls, then known as Brown's Falls (fig. 29). The artist's own words describe both the scene and his drawing of it:

Wandering in another direction . . . my ear caught the music of a cascade, and following the beck of its cadence, I came suddenly upon a high bank, crowned with shrubbery, which overlooked a deep chasm. Into this a clear stream, the outlet of several little lakes, was leaping from the crown of a precipice, about fifty feet in height. Coming upon it so suddenly and unexpectedly, and the bright sun burnishing every ripple and painting an iris upon its front, I stood in mute admiration for a long time, before I could open my portfolio, to tether to paper, as far as possible, the beauty of the cascade.[8]

Hoeffler's sentiments about the beauty of the Minnesota scene were echoed by a much better known American artist, who in the 1850's painted Minnehaha Falls and Lake Pepin. John Frederick Kensett (1816–1872), a Connecticut-born landscapist, was trained as an engraver (as were many important American artists), and his pictures reflect the precision and delicacy of that medium. They also reflect the fascination of many mid-century painters with the scientific and aesthetic properties of light. This interest was, of course, not exclusive to America, but part of a larger artistic awakening to the problems posed by the representation of nature in all her many moods. In Europe the development of photography, on the one hand, and landscape painting, on the other, bears testimony to the nineteenth century's fascination with light. In France, for instance, a group of artists went out to the forests of Barbizon near Fontainebleau to paint from nature in the open air. Their movement led to the Impressionists, whose main preoccupation was the transitory effect of light in nature. In England John Constable and J. M. W. Turner also studied light and atmospheric effects in the rural countryside and on the sea. And, though this relationship is not sufficiently understood, one must not overlook the important part played by Germany, especially by the Dresden artist Caspar David Friedrich, in the development of American romantic landscape painting.

The main body of landscape painting in nineteenth-century America has been called "luminist" because of its portrayal of nature in poetic, light-filled terms.[9] There were emotional as well as pictorial connotations in this tradition. The artists who belonged to it felt a deep personal attachment to the American scene, and they expressed that attachment in a clear, firm naturalism in which light was both the unifying element and the expression of their conscious identification with their native land.

John Kensett was a leader among them. He had lived and sketched in England and on the Continent before returning to America, where he made New York City his home. But eager for new impressions and fresh observations of nature, he traveled widely during the summers, making sketches which he later developed into more finished pictures in his New York studio.[10] One such excursion brought him to the upper Mississippi in the summer of 1854 where he painted two popular Minnesota scenes. The Lake Pepin view, actually titled *View on the Upper Mississippi* (plate 13), is typical of Kensett's simple yet delicate style. In a subtle color harmony of golds, browns, and grays, he evokes a deep, transparent space through which we are transported to a silent, almost uninhabited land. Only a few ducks in the widening river and a group of Indians on the far shore interrupt the tranquil solitude. The smooth, polished surface of the picture leaves no trace of the artist's brush and thus obliterates any reference to his presence. We are left alone in the haunting stillness of a distant frontier.

Kensett's other known Minnesota scene, *Minnehaha Falls* (fig. 30), was given by the artist to his friend Henry Wadsworth Longfellow, whose poem had made the falls world famous. The painting contrasts the darkness of the rocky gorge with the brightness of the falling waters, adding a screen of white birches to emphasize the wilderness locale. Though cool shadows are substituted here for the sunlit clarity of the Lake Pepin scene, the high horizon line and relatively crowded space relate it to the artist's *Cascade in the Forest* of 1852 or *Mountain Stream* of four years later, both of which are typical of the waterfall scenes that are an important part of Kensett's work. Kensett's *Minnehaha Falls* still hangs today in Longfellow's

Fig. 29. Adolf Hoeffler. *Minnehaha Falls*, 1852.
St. Paul. Courtesy of Minnesota Historical Society.
Pencil sketch, 13¾ x 9½ inches.

Fig. 30. John Kensett. *Minnehaha Falls*, c. 1856.
Cambridge, Mass. Longfellow House.
Courtesy of U.S. Department of the Interior. Oil on
board, 11¾ x 9 5/16 inches.

Fig. 31. Jerome B. Thompson. *The Falls of Minnehaha,*
1870. Minneapolis. Courtesy of University of Minnesota Gallery.
Oil on canvas, 24 x 17 inches.

Cambridge, Massachusetts, house, next to a water-color sketch of the same subject by a touring Englishman, Lord Dufferin. For the poet of *Hiawatha,* who himself never visited the site of his poem, these representations of the "Laughing Waters" must have been especially treasured mementos.

Jerome B. Thompson (1814–1886) was a contemporary of John Kensett's, and, like him, an eastern artist who thought Minnehaha Falls (fig. 31) picturesque enough for his brush. Unlike his usual landscapes, which are inhabited by bucolic figures happily at home in nature, Thompson's view of the falls is sunny and colorful but avoids any reference to man's presence. Thompson had studied in England for a number of years in the mid-fifties, and it is possible that he saw and admired there the landscapes of John Constable. Both artists reveal an interest in the glint of light in nature, which they convey through dabs of pure, bright color applied to canvas. This impressionistic technique is more sparklingly evident in Thompson's *Minnehaha Falls* (1870) than it is in his carefully detailed earlier work.

A similar interest in the effects of light in nature, particularly in its more dramatic aspects, distinguishes the art of Albert Bierstadt (1830–1902). The son of German immigrants from Düsseldorf, he went back to his native city to study painting at the academy there from 1853 to 1856. In a sense he belongs to the group of artist-explorers discussed earlier, for when he returned to America he joined Frederick W. Lander's expedition sent by the federal government to map an overland wagon route to the Pacific. He brought back many sketches and a passionate admiration for the grandeur of the American West. He later expressed this admiration in large dramatic landscapes of almost panoramic proportions. These display the precise, tight realism and penchant for theatrical effects that were typical of Düsseldorf-trained artists. But Bierstadt also produced a number of smaller, more loosely painted pictures that reveal a freshness and informality that is lacking in the larger, more pretentious ones.

Bierstadt's Minnesota scenes belong to the simpler, more personal category of his work. He was in the

Fig. 32. Albert Bierstadt. *Clouds over the Prairie*. New York. Courtesy of Kennedy
Galleries, Inc. Oil on paper, 12½ x 19½ inches.

area several times in the 1860's and 1870's, and he left
a number of vivid pictorial records of his visits. One
of these, an early view of Duluth (plate 14), shows
the small town clinging to the hills above Lake Superior. The scattered houses are mostly simple frame
cottages, though the beginnings of industry also appear. It is still a rough pioneer community of dirt
roads and simple wooden bridges, but the clear, sunny light crisply defines the contours of the settlement
and expressively evokes the optimism of a frontier
town.

Bierstadt's painting *Clouds over the Prairie* (fig.
32) also belongs to the smaller, more personal work
of this artist. It is probably a study sketch indicating
Bierstadt's growing interest in the transitory effects
of atmospheric changes in nature, especially in her
more dramatic moments. Through subtle tonal grada-
tions and skillful manipulation of light and shadow,
the artist vividly captures the moving panorama of
changing light.

Even more personal, in terms of the history of the
painting, is Bierstadt's view of Minnehaha Falls (fig.
33). This was painted as a gift for Archie Walker, the
small son of Bierstadt's friend Thomas Barlow Walker,
an early patron of the arts in Minneapolis. It is a small
panel painting, bearing on the back an inscription
dated March 29, 1926. The inscription reads "Painted
for Archie Walker by Albert Bierstadt—August 27,
1886, Archie aged 4 years and 3 months Bierstadt being a guest at our house Cor 8th and Hennepin for 10
days or more as both shown here. T. Walker." Only
Archie is shown, however, as a tiny, straw-hatted figure sitting on the bank of the stream below the falls
(fig. 34). It is a light-filled and lighthearted sketch of
Minnesota's famous landmark and a charming gift for
a little boy who obviously treasured it all his life.

Minnehaha Falls was, in fact, a favorite subject for
the nineteenth-century American landscapist, who
probably drew added inspiration from Longfellow's
poem. In 1862, for example, Robert S. Duncanson

Fig. 33. Albert Bierstadt. *Minnehaha Falls*, 1886.
Forest Hills, New York.
Collection of Ione and Hudson Walker.
Oil on wood panel, 6⅜ x 5⅜ inches.

Fig. 34. Albert Bierstadt. *Minnehaha Falls.*
Detail, 1886. Forest Hills, New York.
Collection of Ione and Hudson Walker.
Oil on wood panel, 6⅜ x 5⅜ inches.

(1817-21–1872) painted *The Falls of Minnehaha* (plate 15), in the rich, decorative style for which he is noted. He may have come up the Mississippi as a steamboat tourist, for he painted another Minnesota tourist attraction, Lake Pepin (fig. 35), along the way.[11] Duncanson's life is fairly well known. He was the son of a mulatto mother and a Scottish father, was brought up in Canada, and joined his mother in Cincinnati around 1841. He exhibited there for the first time in the following year. About 1843 he was commissioned by Nicholas Longworth, a local patron of the arts, to paint a series of eight landscape murals for "Belmont," his home in Cincinnati (now the Taft Museum). Longworth, an active abolitionist, was instrumental in getting the Anti-Slavery League to send Duncanson to Europe to study in 1853. He returned to Europe at least once more, for he was in Britain from 1863 to 1866, at which time he seems to have met the poet Tennyson. In fact, there is something of Tennyson's (and also Longfellow's) imagery in Duncanson's rich masses of foliage, deep atmospheric perspective, and soft, flowing light. A melancholy tinge colors the late afternoon sun that illuminates his *Minnehaha Falls*. It evokes both Longfellow's "forest primeval" and Tennyson's

> . . . cool mosses deep,
> [where] thro' the moss the ivies creep,
> And in the stream the long-leaved flowers
> weep.[12]

The almost mystic reverence for nature that is apparent here is, of course, characteristic of the painters of the Hudson River School, whose work Duncanson undoubtedly knew, either at firsthand or through published reproductions. The lyrical, romantic note they sound goes back in European painting to the airy, glowing landscapes of seventeenth-century France and particularly to those of Claude Lorrain. But, if Lorrain's idyll was a golden utopia peopled by biblical or classical heroes, Duncanson's was a western wilderness inhabited by nature's own nobleman, the American Indian.

It is instructive to compare Duncanson's *Minnehaha Falls* with a painting of the same subject by Joseph

Fig. 35. Robert Duncanson. *Lake Pepin*. Cleveland. Courtesy of Cleveland Museum of Art. Gift of William Macbeth, Inc. Oil on canvas, 12 x 21⅝ inches.

Rusling Meeker (1827–1887), for Meeker's is more spontaneous and less consciously "picturesque." A transplanted easterner, Meeker was born in Newark, New Jersey, reared in Auburn, New York, and educated at the National Academy in New York City. After residing for a while in New York City, Buffalo, and Louisville, Kentucky, he moved to St. Louis in 1859. During the Civil War he served as paymaster in the United States Navy assigned to the Mississippi Squadron. It was there that he began to paint the scenery of the lower Mississippi River, the swamps and bayous dripping with Spanish moss, for which he became known. He painted the upper river, too, on summer excursions he took from St. Louis. An undated painting by him, *Sunset and Moonrise, Lake Pepin, Minnesota,* has much of the romantic aura of his southern landscapes, though another, *Old Lime Kiln, Frontenac, Minnesota,* painted in 1873, is much more matter-of-fact.[13] It is similar in spirit to the artist's *Minnehaha Falls* (fig. 36), which is dated 1879 and which projects an immediacy, a directness, that

is rare in his work. Painted from an oblique vantage point below the falls, Meeker's portrayal is a fresh and spontaneous one. Instead of the rich, golden light of Duncanson's landscape, we have here an impression of intermittent sunlight, shining through green foliage. It flickers on the white trunks of the birches and on the bright cascade of water tumbling into the rocky stream below. In its success in placing us in direct relationship to the scene—rather than at a nostalgic distance from it—the painting captures the same spirit of a fleeting, light-filled moment in time that was the goal of the contemporary French Impressionists.

The same impressionistic quality may be seen in the work of John Severinus Conway (1852–1925). His *Vermillion River near Hastings* (fig. 37) reveals an interest in the natural scene and his ability to capture its fresh vibrant quality in the broad brushstrokes of his compositions. His *View of Fort Snelling* (fig. 38) of 1875 is even more loosely painted, with the result that the brushstrokes themselves create the texture of the picture.[14] Conway was a product of the Chicago

Fig. 36. Joseph Meeker. *Minnehaha Falls*, 1879.
New York. Courtesy of Kennedy
Galleries, Inc. Oil on canvas, 14 x 8 inches.

Art Institute and, during the 1870's, a resident of Milwaukee, Wisconsin. During the summers he, like so many of his colleagues, made extended sketching and painting trips into Minnesota. In 1881, however, he went abroad to study and paint, and it was not till then that he actually saw French Impressionist works firsthand. In spite of his success as a painter, Conway's later career was devoted largely to sculpture.

Another, earlier, tradition in European art whose influence is apparent in American nineteenth-century painting and, therefore, evident in the work of the itinerant landscapists who visited Minnesota in the early days of its statehood is that of seventeenth-century Holland. Similarities in the history of the Dutch in the seventeenth century and the Americans in the nineteenth are interesting and relevant. Both of them, recently liberated from a foreign yoke and proud of their new independence, were imbued with a passionate patriotism that led to descriptions of each country, at least in visual terms, as a new Eden. Thus, Thomas Prichard Rossiter's *Minnesota Prairie* (plate 16), painted in 1865, bears more than a coincidental resemblance to the broad and peaceful country landscapes of the van Ruisdaels and Meindert Hobbema.

Rossiter (1818–1871) was a New York–based painter who had established a small reputation for himself as a landscape and history painter. In 1840 he and two friends, John Kensett and John W. Casilear, embarked from New York on a leisurely tour of Europe. All three were protégés of Asher B. Durand, a leader, with Thomas Cole, of the Hudson River School, and their fellow passenger on the *British Queen*. Rossiter later traveled through Switzerland with Cole himself. He resided in Paris during the 1840's and in Rome in the 1850's before returning to America in 1856, well schooled in the European landscape tradition.

Rossiter's portrayal of rural Minnesota right after the Civil War is similar to Dutch seventeenth-century landscapes primarily in its celebration of the simple, pastoral life represented by a broad sweep of peaceful countryside. As in the Dutch tradition, the transparent space is emphasized by a low horizon line. Moreover, this landscape is inhabited by farmers, settled tillers of the soil, and no longer by the wild, free,

Fig. 37. John S. Conway. *Vermillion River near Hastings*, 1874. New York. Courtesy of
Kennedy Galleries, Inc. Oil on paper, 9½ x 13¼ inches.

"uncivilized" noble savage. According to the nineteenth century's cultural view, "natural" virtue was still inherent in the American farmer (as it had also been in the Dutch peasant), but it was natural virtue tempered now by a measure of unsophisticated, therefore uncorrupted, civilization. Pictorially this attitude is reflected in the small cow shed, plank bridge, hay ricks, and rustic cottage all attesting to the simple, unspoiled life of the American yeoman farmer. The golden light that shines down on the scene, from a vast, expansive sky, further blesses his industry and virtue.

The "picturesque" Indian as a subject for the artist had not yet, however, entirely disappeared. Thomas Waterman Wood (1823–1903) of Montpelier, Vermont, and later of New York City painted Little Crow (plate 17), a Sioux Indian boy, while visiting at Fort Snelling in 1862. The picture is reminiscent of Seth Eastman's *Indian on the Lookout,* and indeed one may wonder if Wood saw the Eastman picture, or at least preparatory sketches for it, while he was at the fort. In any event Wood, an artist known for his scenes of country life and of picturesque types, chose, significantly, not an Indian brave but an Indian child dressed as a brave for his subject. Eastman never indulged in the type of sentimentality implicit in Wood's preference for children, women, and old men as his models, for though Eastman's attitude toward the Indians was colored by the romanticism of his age, it was modified by a genuine interest in a way of life that was rapidly disappearing.

Most of the tourist-artists who came to Minnesota in the 1860's and 1870's, however, were landscapists who were more attracted to the natural scene than to full-scale portraits of Indians. In the summer of 1866, four years after Thomas Waterman Wood's portrayal of an Indian boy at Fort Snelling, Alfred Thompson Bricher (1837–1908) traveled up the Mississippi to sketch the river scenery. Little is known of Bricher's early life except that he was born in Portsmouth, New Hampshire, in 1837, that he attended schools in Newburyport, Massachusetts, and that after clerking in a dry goods store in Boston (where he may also have attended classes at the Lowell Institute) he decided, in 1858, to become a professional artist.

Bricher seems to have been attracted to the romance of the West from his early youth, for his first known work is *Landscape with Indians,* dated 1856.[15] In his own words, it was a "fantasie," a term he used to describe several of his early drawings. He soon abandoned pure flights of imagination in favor of landscapes more familiar to him, such as New York's Catskill Mountains or the New England shore. Nevertheless, in 1866 he embarked on a Mississippi River steamboat, sketching first the scenery at Dubuque, Iowa, then Prairie du Chien, and, about June 22, the shore scene at Red Wing. Though he did not refer to Lake Pepin in his written notes, he apparently sketched there, too, for in 1870 he exhibited two oil paintings of this area at the National Academy: *On the Mississippi, near La Crosse, Wisconsin—Shower Clearing* and *The Maiden's Rock, Lake Pepin, Mississippi River.*[16] He did not stay in the upper Middle West for long. By August, 1866, he was back in the East, packing up his Boston studio and establishing himself in the more challenging artistic climate of New York City. There he continued to paint in the tradition of Kensett and other "luminists" of the Hudson River School.

There were, of course, some touring artists who, though competent painters, were obscure in their own day and are almost completely forgotten today. They came to Minnesota, painted a few landscapes, and then continued on their travels west or returned to their homes in the East. One of these forgotten tourists is Ferdinand Reichardt (1819–1895), who painted *St. Anthony Falls* in 1857 (fig. 39). He was a Danish landscape painter, born in Breda, who made a modest name for himself with a number of paintings of Niagara Falls. It is known that he had a studio in New York City from 1856 to 1859, that he exhibited at the National Academy of Design in 1858, and that he died in Oakland, California, in 1895. Somewhere along the way he stopped in Minneapolis long enough to paint the Falls of St. Anthony in a style that reflects the precise, hard drawing of the Düsseldorf Academy. It is not known how long he stayed in Minnesota and what, if any, was his influence on the art of the new state.

Another, even more obscure, tourist was S. Holmes

Fig. 38. John S. Conway. *View of Fort Snelling*, 1875. New York. Courtesy of Kennedy Galleries, Inc. Oil on canvas on board, 7 x 13 inches.

Fig. 39. Ferdinand Reichardt. *St. Anthony Falls*, 1857. St. Paul. Courtesy of Minnesota Historical Society. Oil on canvas, 16 x 26 inches.

Andrews. It is known only that he exhibited at the National Academy of Design in 1843 and that at that time he was living in New York City. This may be the same Andrews who exhibited a panorama of the Great West in Philadelphia and other eastern cities in 1856. A picture he painted of the pioneer town of St. Paul in 1855 (fig. 40) may well have been intended as a study for that panorama. It is even more clear and linear than the Reichardt painting, and its presentation of minute details of locale—as well as its stage-scenery style—relates it to the work of the panorama painters, for whose audiences a view of the enormous canvas was the next best thing to being there.

Most of the painters discussed so far were artists of some degree of skill and sophistication who considered themselves professionals in the arts. There were others, however, who traveled through Minnesota in its early years, illustrating its scenery in a more naive and unpretentious style. They stand somewhere between the professional artists who came to the area in search of the picturesque wilderness of the American frontier and the unschooled primitives who were soon to be found among the settlers themselves. These painters described what they saw with an unpretentious realism that earned them no lasting artistic reputations but did leave a clear and vivid picture of pioneer Minnesota.

Edwin Whitefield (1816–1892) was one such traveler. He first came to the area in the summer of 1855 and found, to his disappointment, that frontier Minnesota was not quite as picturesque as he had been led to believe. However, the place grew on him enough to attract him back the following summer. At that time he added a view of the Falls of St. Anthony flanked by Minneapolis and St. Paul (fig. 41) to his album of lithographed views of North American cities. When his *View of St. Anthony, Minneapolis and St. Anthony Falls* was published in 1857, it was endorsed with a local editor's comment that it not only was appropriate "for parlor ornament or for a gift" but would also be "of historic interest a few years hence."[17] Meanwhile, Whitefield had become in-

volved in a promotional venture to advertise pictorially the town sites that were springing up on the Minnesota frontier. During the late 1850's, his lithographed views, based on water-color originals (fig. 42), were widely distributed by land promoters to attract settlers to the area. They were also used to illustrate Whitefield's popular articles and lectures on the attractions of life in Minnesota.

Whitefield was not an amateur in either land promotion or art. Born and educated in England, he had speculated in Canadian real estate and after 1840 had established himself as a landscapist in Boston and New York. He specialized in lithographed city views but, at the same time, illustrated a book on American wild flowers. His versatile talents were admirably suited to the promotional work he undertook for the new state of Minnesota.

Two of Whitefield's water colors, *First View of Fairy Lake* (plate 18) and the picture of his own home, *Kandotta* (fig. 43), where he resided in the late 1850's, are typical of his style. They are unpretentious genre descriptions of everyday life in the new state, imbued with the cheerful optimism appropriate to promotional illustration: clear blues and greens predominate, punctuated by an occasional note of bright red or yellow. The paintings lack the dramatic overtones of the more ambitious landscapes we have seen; instead they describe life in Minnesota as sunny, uncomplicated, and pleasant. But, though Whitefield continued to advertise the area in words and pictures, promising that "families that a few years previously were toiling for a pitiful subsistence in the crowded Atlantic towns, [would] find themselves in their new homes . . . enjoying the luxuries and refinements of the most happy civilization,"[18] his efforts to promote a settlers' haven brought him neither personal recognition nor financial reward. In 1860 he left Minnesota for Chicago, where he added to his city views. Four years later he settled permanently in Massachusetts. He died near Boston in 1892, still looking back longingly on his pioneering experiences as a commercial artist for the new state of Minnesota.

Fig. 40. S. Holmes Andrews. *St. Paul*, 1855. St. Paul. Courtesy of Minnesota
Historical Society. Oil on canvas, 15 x 26 inches.

Fig. 41.
Edwin Whitefield. *View
of Falls of St. Anthony*, 1856.
St. Paul. Courtesy of Minnesota
Historical Society. Water
color, 9 x 13½ inches.

Fig. 42.
Edwin Whitefield.
View of Homer, Minnesota, c. 1858.
St. Paul. Courtesy of Minnesota
Historical Society.
Water color, 6 x 9 inches.

Fig. 43.
Edwin Whitefield.
Kandotta, November, 1857.
St. Paul. Courtesy
of Minnesota Historical Society.
Water color, 5½ x 8½ inches.

V Settlers: The Primitives

In the early days of Minnesota's history, the land itself, as well as its colorful, native inhabitants, attracted both exploring artists and touring ones. They wanted to capture a picture of a vanishing frontier, a fleeting moment in our national story, before it disappeared forever in the advance of white civilization. Once the state was well established, however, and settlers began to replace soldiers, explorers, and adventurers, the art produced by and for them changed as well. For one thing, portrait painting began to assume a new importance. Settled people wanted pictures of themselves and their relatives to hand down to their descendants, and before the perfection and spread of photography, painted portraits were the only means of assuring this sort of visual memory. Secondly, genre painting, the representation of everyday life, began to replace the popularity of the romantic frontier as a subject for the artist's brush. For those who lived there, the frontier was not all that romantic. It was simply their home, the setting of their ordinary lives, and they were just as eager as their countrymen in the East to see that life reflected in genre and narrative painting. Landscapes continued to be painted, of course, but they lost something of the dramatic, wilderness aspect of the Hudson River School and became instead straightforward portrayals of familiar places. Thirdly, as churches were established in settled com-

munities and their congregations grew, religious art appeared to decorate both those churches and the settlers' own homes. Finally, there began to appear another art form, or medium—one that was not produced by itinerant artists. That was, of course, sculpture, which, because it is much more expensive and less portable than paint and canvas, depends on settled communities and established practitioners in order to flourish.

The ethnic character of the settled communities had an effect on their art as well. It is important to remember that the art of the explorers and soldiers first and the tourists later was one that reflected, by and large, the art of the eastern seaboard of the United States. To be sure, that in turn was formed by European conventions, especially those of England, France, and Germany. These influences, however, were filtered through our national experience to become what has been called the American tradition in art. But the art of the settlers began to reflect, more directly than previously, their ethnic backgrounds. The German immigrants who flocked to this country following the revolution of 1848 were among the first to form a solid ethnic community in Minnesota. The Irish also came early and were followed by waves of immigrants from Norway, Sweden, and other Scandinavian countries. As the contagion of "America Fever" spread, others of

Europe's "tired, [its] poor, [its] huddled masses yearning to breathe free"[1] came to Minnesota and were soon assimilated. Interestingly, it was the Norwegians who maintained the strongest artistic ties to their homeland and best preserved their own traditions in the new land.

For purposes of convenience and clarity, the work of the professional artists will be discussed separately from that of the primitive, frequently amateur artists whose work, though not inferior, must be judged by different aesthetic standards. Sometimes the distinction is hard to make and the two categories occasionally overlap. Nevertheless, there is a difference and each, in its own way, has much to tell us about the development of art produced by and for Minnesotans in the first half-century of their statehood.

By the very nature of their status as amateurs, most of the "primitives" are little known, and frequently even anonymous, artists. They were self-taught painters and sculptors whose main business in life—at least in respect to earning a living—was something other than the practice of art. Even when we know the names of these obscure artists, we know very little else about them, for they rarely held exhibitions of their work or joined the artistic establishment. Stylistically, their work is distinguished by a direct approach to visual reality and its representation in naive and literal terms. These terms usually ignore a central focus which subordinates some elements in a composition in order to emphasize others. Primitive artists also ignore academic rules of linear or atmospheric perspective and produce flat, decorative compositions in which pattern and color assume an ornamental purpose of their own.

One such primitive painting is the early view of Homer, Minnesota, painted about 1869 by an obscure artist named John T. Sperry (fig. 44). In the typical manner of the primitive painter, all the objects in the picture—houses, trees, people, the steamboat and barge in the river—are given equal importance. Their scale, in relation to one another, is determined by their decorative function and not their representational one. The scene is dominated by the distinctive moundlike

hill in the center, around and upon which objects are neatly arranged. The houses cling, or rather hang on, to the hill as though they were paper cutouts pasted upon it. There is no attempt either at suggesting their solid, three-dimensional quality or at modeling them through the manipulation of light and shadow. Neither is there any attempt at linear perspective. Some of the features, the fenced yards and the barge, for instance, are shown in a bird's-eye view, as though we were flying directly over them. Nevertheless, the artist has managed to suggest a cold and windy day. A strong gust catches at the dress and scarf of the lady who has climbed to the top of the hill with her gentleman companion, and the bare trees and stark landscape emphasize the chilly climate. The two figures form the apex of the composition which is aesthetically successful precisely because of its direct and unselfconscious style and its carefully balanced pattern of line, shape, and color.

The same aesthetic principles apply to a small picture of Beaver Bay (fig. 45) painted in 1869 by Mrs. J. J. Lowry. It illustrates another pioneer Minnesota community, this one on the north shore of Lake Superior. Mrs. Lowry, who was the wife of the local schoolteacher, painted at least five of these Beaver Bay scenes in the same way that Sergeant Thomas of Fort Snelling had earlier painted several versions of his familiar surroundings. Even though Mrs. Lowry was also undoubtedly self-taught, her painting is much more academically sophisticated than John T. Sperry's. She still "enumerates" objects in the upended perspective of the primitive painter but succeeds better than Sperry in indicating space. The houses and trees in the background are smaller than those in the foreground, and the schooner, *Charley*, which is preparing to dock, is much more correctly scaled in reference to the total composition. A barn, a general store, and Mr. Lowry's schoolhouse flank the road, while partly visible above the lower frame are the houses of the settlers. All are presented with equal emphasis in what is essentially a literal description of early Beaver Bay.

St. Columkill's Catholic Church in Belle Creek (fig. 46), by Michael McAleavy, also spreads the objects

Fig. 44. John T. Sperry. *Homer, Minnesota*, c. 1869. Cooperstown. Courtesy of New York State Historical Society. Water color, 17 x 14¼ inches.

out in a bird's-eye view of the scene. The houses, barns, animals, and especially the impressive brick church are all placed neatly in the composition. Though the church is placed off-center, its size and detail indicate its important role in the life of the tiny community. The white snow and gray skies provide a perfect foil for the strong, bright colors of the objects in the composition—the church, houses, and animals— and emphasize their decorative purpose. The colors also convey, in a way hardly surpassed by more so- phisticated pictures, the unique quality of Minnesota's weather.

That same cold light that suggests so well the qual- ity of Minnesota's winter climate is evident in an even earlier primitive painting called *St. Anthony Falls* (fig. 47) and signed "J. R. Sloan, 1856" on the back. The artist should not be confused, however, with Ju- nius R. Sloan (1827–1900), a well-known Ohio-born painter who, like Duncanson, worked in the tradition of the Hudson River School but resided most of his life in the Middle West. Junius Sloan is not known to have visited Minnesota, but even if he did, his style was much too refined and atmospheric to be confused with that of the primitive *St. Anthony Falls*. The painting is by an amateur artist whose main emphasis is on the colorful contrast between the stark, icy winter land- scape and the colorful robes of the two Indians con- versing in the foreground. The houses of the small set- tlement of St. Anthony dot the riverbank on the right, while in the center rises a tall, stark tree inhabited by a single black bird perched on its branches. It is a typical primitive landscape, naive in its expression of scale and perspective, colorful rather than sculptural in its representation of form, and more successful in achieving a sense of decorative pattern than in con- veying an illusion of the real world.

Fig. 45.
Mrs. J. J. Lowry.
Beaver Bay, 1869. Duluth.
Courtesy of St. Louis County
Historical Society.
Oil on canvas, 13¼ x 19 inches.

Fig. 46. Michael McAleavy. *St. Columkill's Catholic Church in Belle Creek,* c. 1900.
Red Wing. Courtesy of Goodhue County Historical Society. Oil on canvas, 18 x 36 inches.

Not quite so primitive, yet still lacking the easy competence of the true professional, is the work of Jonas Holland Howe (1821–1898), a founder of the township of Plymouth, Minnesota.[2] Howe was a civic-minded person, much involved in local politics. He served a term in the state legislature in 1866 and was a friend and co-worker of Ignatius Donnelly, the Populist leader. Howe was born in Petersham, Massachusetts, and was a cousin of George Fuller, whose Minnesota sketches are mentioned in chapter IV. Perhaps upon the recommendation of his cousin, Howe moved to Minnesota in 1854 in search of a healthy and invigorating climate as a cure for the chronic ill health from which he suffered. Though, like Fuller, Howe took up farming as a full-time occupation, he continued to paint pictures too. He never quite achieved, however, the skill and sophistication of his cousin's later work. The paintings that survive are mostly copies of currently popular prints or engravings, such as *Indian Girl Crossing a Stream* or *Bay of Naples at Sunset.* One, however, entitled *The Artist's Paradise* (fig. 48), is probably Howe's response to his own surround-

Fig. 47. J. R. Sloan. *St. Anthony Falls,* 1852. St. Paul.
Courtesy of Minnesota Historical Society.
Oil on canvas, 17 x 19 inches.

Fig. 48. Jonas Holland Howe. *The Artist's Paradise*. Minneapolis. Courtesy of Hennepin
County Historical Society. Oil on canvas, 18 x 24 inches.

ings. The artist is shown contemplating a calm lakeside scene, in a subdued color scheme of greens and browns. Though the technical aspects of perspective and three-dimensional form are understood, the static quality of the composition and its rather literal description of man and nature relate it to primitive painting rather than to academic art.

The Mississippi River and the boats upon it were the frequent subjects of the primitive and the not-so-primitive artist. One of the most delightful works of the former is the painting done in 1895 by one S. J. Durran entitled *Sunday Afternoon on the Levee* (plate 19). Again we see the unfocused composition and the bright, flat colors of the unsophisticated artist, as well as an emphasis on narrative detail. Dr. J. G. Tweedy, a Winona doctor, and the local pharmacist are shown at the right being swamped in the wake of a passing steamboat. According to the story, they had rowed out on the river to wave to the young ladies on the passing steamboat *Pittsburgh* but were dumped unceremoniously into the river instead. They had to swim back to shore, suffering only in their injured dignity. Durran, about whom little is known beyond the fact that he was Dr. Tweedy's patient, has included at the left the old wagon bridge built in 1892 across the Mississippi and demolished in 1943. Whatever the picture may lack in accurate perspective and scale is made up for in the sweeping design of its winding roadway, whose rhythmic curves tie it both literally and visually to the distant hills. In the same way the pattern of the bridge's iron trusses repeats the lacy cast iron balustrades on the steamboat and its large, revolving paddle wheel. The flat, silhouetted forms of the crowd on the shore and the single horse-drawn carriage complete both the story and its ornamental design and place the picture squarely in the best tradition of American primitive painting.

The importance to Winona of the river is emphasized in other pictures as well. The town was one of Minnesota's first permanent settlements by virtue of the fact that it was an early river port. It was founded in 1851 by Captain Orin Smith of the *Nominee*, who was having trouble getting firewood to fuel his steamboat. He reasoned that a port town at Winona's location would provide a population willing to cut cordwood for the passing steamboats, to their mutual benefit. It happened just that way, and Winona grew and prospered as an important steamboat stop on the river.

The painting of Winona in 1867 (fig. 49) by an anonymous artist shows the *Keokuk* and the *Philip Sheridan*, which had regular routes on the Mississippi in the 1860's. It shows, too, that in spite of the increasing use of steamboats on the western rivers, older methods of transportation lingered on. A log raft is seen in the foreground, one that had probably floated or been poled all the way from the lumber country along Wisconsin's Chippewa River to the Mississippi. The broad reaches of the mighty river are suggested in the wide perspective of the picture, the low horizon line, and the sense of deep, expansive space.

The river, and the towns along it, continued to attract untrained artists as well as professional touring artists from the East. An anonymous painter's *Early Settlement on the River* (fig. 50) shows the area around Winona, identifiable by the distinctive shape of the river bluffs. The flat-topped hills tower above the tiny settlement nestled at their base and by their forbidding size seem to emphasize its isolation in a distant wilderness.

By the 1860's, however, rail transportation began to supplement steamboat routes, connecting the river to inland towns and villages. An interesting water color of a steamboat at Fischer's Landing, Minnesota, illustrates this link. It was painted by a visiting English lord, the Marquess of Dufferin and Ava (Frederick Temple Hamilton Blackwood) (1826–1902), who traveled up the river on such a boat. The painting shows a few railroad carriages and an engine drawn up on the riverbank and waiting for the disembarking steamboat passengers. Lord Dufferin continued up the river, sketching the Minnesota scene, and his water-color picture of Minnehaha Falls hangs in Longfellow's Cambridge, Massachusetts, house next to the oil painting of the same subject by John Kensett, which has already been described.

Fig. 49.
Anon. *Winona in 1867*. Winona.
Courtesy of Winona County
Historical Society. Oil on
canvas, 30¼ x 49½ inches.

Fig. 50.
Anon. *Early Settlement on
the River*. Winona. Courtesy of
Winona County Historical Society.
Oil on canvas, 21 x 27 inches.

Fig. 51.
Sergeant James G. McGrew.
Fort Ridgely, Minnesota, 1890.
St. Paul. Courtesy of
Minnesota Historical Society.
Oil on canvas, 28⅛ x 48¼ inches.

One other Winona landscape of this period properly fits into our discussion here even though it does not concentrate on the river itself. *View of Winona in 1867* (plate 20), signed simply Sederberg shows a distant view of Winona from the hills northwest of the town. The artist is probably Alfred Sederberg, who is listed in the Minneapolis city directory of 1871–1872 as "an artist in oil." In his picture of Winona the distinctive chimney-shaped bluffs identify the site and the prosperous town on the river plain below, but the emphasis now is on the tranquil enjoyment of nature and the pleasant out-of-doors. Three strollers, a gentleman and two ladies, rest in the shade of a tree at the left and contemplate the peaceful scene before them. It is a view that illustrates the nineteenth century's optimistic attitude toward the growing industrialization of America—as evidenced by the smoking factory chimneys in the distant town—while retaining an appreciation for the quiet and serenity of the rural scene as well. In a sense, it is a provincial reflection of a well-known American painting of a decade ear-

lier, George Inness's *Lackawanna Valley*, which similarly, though perhaps not so optimistically, depicts the encroachment of industrialization (the railroad train) on rural America.

An interest in narrative detail, also typical of primitive painting, is to be found in a picture entitled *Fort Ridgely, Minnesota* (fig. 51), by an unknown amateur, Sergeant James G. McGrew (d. 1907). He was probably a soldier stationed at the fort, and when he produced this picture in 1890, he drew on one of the most colorful episodes of its past history. The scene represents the burning of Fort Ridgely at the time of the Sioux uprising in 1862, an event still vivid in the memories of many old timers. The buildings of the fort are shown with great precision, correct in scale, but unsoftened by the haze of atmospheric perspective with which nature veils distant objects. The great expanse of empty space suggests the wide flat plains of central Minnesota. It also evokes a sense of peace and false tranquillity, for flames burst rather suddenly, as it seems, from the foreground buildings. The danger and violence they imply seem somehow unreal in the clarity and expansiveness of McGrew's landscape.

Danger and violence, though this time of nature's making, are also vividly suggested in Julius Holm's *Tornado over St. Paul* (fig. 52) of 1893. Holm is still another artist about whom very little is known, but the sharply object-focused quality of his work underlines his status as an amateur, or primitive, painter. The crowdedness of Holm's picture is in marked contrast with the space of McGrew's, though each expresses the real environment it represents. Fort Ridgely does, after all, occupy a considerable area in central Minnesota, while St. Paul, even in 1893, was a built-up city. In keeping with the literal description typical of a primitive painting, several architectural landmarks can be identified in *Tornado over St. Paul*. Prominent on the left are the twin towers of the Church of the Ascension, built in 1871 and still standing today. Over all hovers the ominous black cloud with its tornado funnel, appearing like an apparition of destruction above the roofs of the city. The menace it implies is emphasized by the dark, yellowish light that casts a sulfurous haze over the scene. All who are familiar with tornado weather have experienced this. But however successfully the specific place and particular atmospheric conditions have been presented, the picture still retains the patterned structure and clear narrative quality of the typical primitive painting.

A different but very large category of primitive art is portrait painting. Americans, from the very beginnings of their history, valued this aspect of representational art and encouraged its practitioners, both naive and sophisticated, to produce these tangible examples of their individual lives. Often such portraits were painted by itinerant "limners" who wandered through the towns and villages of rural America with their paints and canvases tucked into their baggage. A knock on the door of a lonely farmhouse resulted often enough in a commission to paint the family then and there with payment frequently in the form of board and lodging. Though these limners usually identified their sitters, they rarely signed their own names and are, therefore, often anonymous participants in the history of American art. We know better the names of artists who were permanent settlers of their towns, though they may have been just as naive as the itinerant ones. Many of the settled primitive artists were women, partly because the life of a traveling painter was not possible for them and partly because young ladies were encouraged to practice art as part of their female accomplishments. So they stayed at home, painting their friends and relatives, and occasionally achieving enough proficiency to be considered professional rather than naive artists.

A typical, and also delightful, example of a naive Minnesota portrait is *Aunt Catherine* (fig. 53), painted about 1870 by Mrs. Edward Ely. Mrs. Ely was the wife of Winona's first minister, and her sitter, Ann Catherine Goddard Smith, was the first white woman settler there. The portrait's hard drawing and emphasis on linear rather than three-dimensional form label it a primitive picture. The prim dress and prim demeanor are also typical. So is the ornamental pattern of the lace collar held together by a cameo broach bearing the miniature likeness of Aunt Catherine's son, who had been the first white baby born in Winona. Primitive portraitists, it can be seen, shared the anecdotal, or narrative, interests of their landscape-painting colleagues.

Some years later, Mrs. Ely painted the portrait of Mr. Mayberry, (fig. 54), the architect of the Winona County Courthouse. It displays a more sophisticated understanding of the three-dimensional modeling of form, but it is debatable whether the technical improvement of the Mayberry portrait projects any more clearly than *Aunt Catherine* the personality and unique individual presence of the sitter.

One other category of Minnesota art, namely primitive religious painting, is represented by a unique example that has recently come to light in a small town in northern Minnesota.[3] An altarpiece representing the Last Supper (plate 21) was painted by John A. Rein in 1895 for the Rose Church in Old Greenbush, near Roseau, Minnesota. Little is yet known about Rein except that he was a local carpenter, that he was a good fiddler,[4] and that this altarpiece is the first of

Fig. 52. Julius Holm. *Tornado over St. Paul*, 1893. Private collection. Oil on canvas, 30¼ x 49¼ inches.

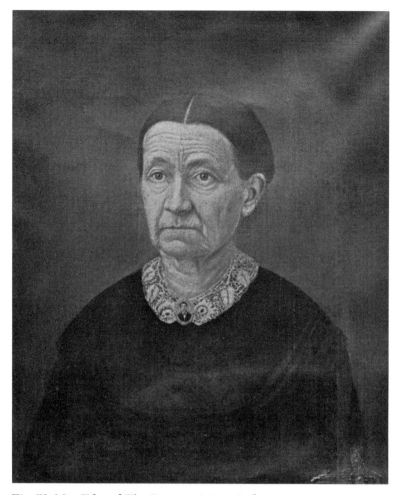

Fig. 53. Mrs. Edward Ely. *Portrait of Aunt Catherine,*
c. 1870. Winona. Courtesy of
Winona County Historical Society. Oil on canvas, 24½ x 20 inches.

several that he painted for the local churches. The others have unfortunately disappeared, but in the memories of some old timers the later ones showed considerable improvement (by which was probably meant greater academic sophistication).

The painting is interesting iconographically in that it shows the apostles grouped around a square table in the old medieval tradition of Last Supper scenes. Renaissance and later representations of the Last Supper usually show the entire group arranged on the far side of a long table placed horizontally across the picture plane with Judas sometimes isolated in the foreground. Prominent in Rein's picture are a basin and ewer. These are symbols of the Washing of the Feet before the Last Supper and the Passion of Christ. The meal takes place in a simple room, not unlike the interiors of the immigrant's own wooden churches, and one of the disciples, in the left foreground, even sits in a typical pioneer chair. Next to him, facing the observer, is Judas, holding up a moneybag for all to see.

The stiff and awkward poses of the figures are characteristically primitive, and so is the confusion the artist shows between profile and frontal views. The beams of the ceiling and the planks in the floor recede into the distance in a studied attempt at linear perspective, but the group is still crowded into the upended space of the simple room. The ceiling beams also serve a symbolic purpose as they radiate outward above the head of Christ, for they suggest rays of light—the actual origin of the halo. Christ's centrality in the pictorial scheme is further stressed by the hanging lamp situated directly above his head, but the apostle John is given strong secondary emphasis by the arched doorway behind him. The group is brightly illuminated by the lamp, which casts a strong shadow on the wooden floor and repeats the curvilinear shape of the basin and ewer in the foreground. It would be interesting to find the source of the artist's unusual iconography and to see whether it was modified in his later, lost altarpieces. Until they, or others like them, come to light, however, the Rein altarpiece constitutes tantalizing evidence of the presence and strength of primitive religious painting in Minnesota.

Religious art in Minnesota was more frequently expressed in sculpture than in painting, though sculpture, for a variety of reasons that have already been noted, did not become a frequent art form in the state until well into the twentieth century. Nevertheless, some sculpture did exist, usually growing out of the woodcarving tradition of the immigrant furniture makers. In at least one case it produced a major monument of early Minnesotan, and indeed of American, primitive sculpture.

Between 1897 and 1904, a Benson Minnesota farmer named Lars Christenson (1839–1910) carved a large wooden altarpiece for his church (plate 22).[5] Christenson had immigrated to Benson from Sogndal, Norway, in 1866, bringing with him Norway's old tradition of woodcarving and fine cabinetwork. The form of the altarpiece is based on the medieval and Renaissance triptych—a three-paneled (usually painted) altarpiece with a large central scene and narrower side panels on hinges, which could be folded over it. Baroque adaptations in carved wood were common in the parish churches of Norway, and though Christenson had been in America for over thirty years when he began his masterwork, he must have retained some memory of them. He freely adapted, however, both the form of his altarpiece and the models for the figures in it to fit his own decorative purposes and strong sense of design. The pictured scenes were actually based on the realistic illustrations in a Norwegian Bible printed in America in 1890.[6] In the carved altarpiece, however, the disposition of the figures and the style in which they are represented are based not on any attempt to create the illusion of reality but rather on the abstract principles of decoration and symbolic composition. Thus, in typically primitive fashion, the artist arranges the figures in the panels according to their relative importance in the narrative and their schematic relationship to each other. If the figures do not conform to correct scale or indicate realistic spatial relationships, they do succeed in focusing attention on the central scene, which is already emphasized by the relative austerity of its background and the exaggerated size of the figure of Christ on the cross. Here, as elsewhere in the altarpiece, anatomical features are treated decoratively, the folds of the loin cloth, for instance, repeating the striations of the rib cage and even reflecting the patterns of the wood

Fig. 54. Mrs. Edward Ely. *Portrait of Mr. Mayberry*, c. 1875. Winona. Courtesy of Winona County Historical Society. Oil on canvas, 24 x 20 inches.

Fig. 55. Lars Christenson. Detail from *Altarpiece. The Nativity*, 1897–1904.
Decorah, Ia. Courtesy of Norwegian-American Museum. Luther College Collection.
Wood, 18 x 24¼ inches.

grain on the panel itself. The side panel illustrating the Nativity (fig. 55) is carved in a curious form of recessed relief in which the disembodied heads of the worshiping shepherds float above Mary, who is displaying the infant Jesus in the manger. Separating and surrounding the narrative panels is an intricate framework of columns, finials, garlands, and curving tendrils which add richness to the altarpiece and contrast to the abstract simplicity of the figured scenes.

Christenson never finished the altarpiece. Disillusioned when it was rejected by the congregation for whom it was intended, the artist left the three lower panels empty. It was exhibited at the Minnesota State Fair in 1904 and then stored away until Christenson's death in 1910. Now in the collection of the Norwegian-American Museum in Decorah, Iowa, it is recognized as an outstanding example of folk art in America.

The relationship between fine cabinetwork and carved church ornamentation is central to an understanding of the type of sculpture produced in the early years of Minnesota history. Peter Eich (1834–1920), for example, was among the men from nearby farms who worked for many years in the carpentry workshop at St. John's Abbey in Collegeville, Minnesota. There he built many pieces of furniture for the monastery and the church, as well as assisting with the building of shops, a farm, and the college. In 1874 he also made the painted wooden shrine in figure 56. The same tradition of fine craftsmanship that characterizes Lars Christenson's altarpiece is present in this work as well. Though not as elaborate or ambitious as the Decorah piece, it betrays a similar dependence on the persistent traditions of baroque design. Slim, graceful columns topped by cross-shaped finials, shell arches, and abstract patterns create a rich and harmonious design, while the Christian symbols of the wine and the sheaf of wheat decorate the side panels in their cusped arch niches. In the Christenson altarpiece, the natural shades of the various woods create a rich, coloristic pattern; but Eich, conforming more closely than Christenson to the tradition of folk art, painted his carved wooden shrine. It is a work whose purpose, while primarily utilitarian, rises above mere serviceability to express the creative urge of the true artist.

Fig. 56. Peter Eich. *Shrine*, 1874. Private collection. Gilded and painted wood, 60 x 38 inches.

VI Settlers: The Professionals

Training, or the lack of it, in an art school or academy is one of the accepted criteria for distinguishing the professional from a primitive or folk artist. This is confusing, however, because some of America's greatest artists, John Singleton Copley, for instance, were largely self-taught. Sometimes, then, it is a matter of technical skill or sophistication that determines the separation between primitive and professional; but here, too, the division is marked by a thin and unclear line. Perhaps the attitude of the artist himself is the best measure of his professionalism, for most academic artists aspire to tangible signs of reward from their peers in the academy, while folk artists usually do not. Whatever the criteria of judgment are, however, one can safely say that professional, *resident* artists began to appear among Minnesota's settlers as early as the first years of its statehood.

In 1857, for example, an artist by the name of Ben Cooley was mentioned in James Goodhue's newspaper, *Minnesota Pioneer*, as a resident of St. Paul and a professional painter. His portrait of David Olmstead, St. Paul's first mayor, hangs today in the Minnesota Historical Society building as testimony to the degree of professionalism present among Minnesota's early portraitists. Cooley probably arrived in Minnesota from Kalamazoo, Michigan, where he maintained a portrait studio in the 1840's and again in the 1870's and where a number of his works still exist. Though

he primarily painted portraits, including one of Governor Stephen Miller in 1865, he also exhibited *Deer Chased by Wolves* in the state fair of that year.

There were others who followed. In 1858 Alvah Bradish (1806–1901), professor of art at the University of Michigan, established residence in St. Paul long enough to paint fifteen to twenty portraits and returned in 1876 to portray Governor Cushman K. Davis and Bishop Henry B. Whipple of Faribault. In 1863 a New York portrait and landscape painter named Bartlett attempted to establish a studio and art school, but he gave up in April, 1864, and vanished into the obscurity from which he had come. Charles (Carl) Gutherz (1844–1907) arrived on the scene in 1873, after studying and exhibiting abroad, and though he is more closely identified with St. Louis where he was a professor of fine arts at Washington University, he established a St. Paul studio and painted allegorical pictures and portraits of Minnesota's governors. At about the same time, the first Minnesota-born artist, Frank Bass (b. 1848), returned from a period of study in Paris, opened a studio in St. Paul, and offered to give instruction in drawing and painting. In 1878 he and others attempted unsuccessfully to establish an art academy in St. Paul. Discouraged by its failure, he abandoned art, consoling himself thereafter in the comfort of a successful real estate business.

Minnesota does not, then, seem to have been very

Plate 20. Alfred Sederberg. *View of Winona in 1867*. Winona. Courtesy of Winona
County Historical Society. Oil on canvas, 28¼ x 44¼ inches.

Plate 21. John A. Rein. *Altarpiece: The Last Supper*, 1895.
Roseau. Courtesy of Roseau County Historical
Society and Museum. Oil on canvas, 78¼ x 33⅛ inches.

Plate 22. Lars Christenson. *Altarpiece: The Crucifixion*, 1897–1904. Decorah, Ia.
Courtesy of Norwegian-American Museum. Luther College Collection.
Wood, 12 feet 7½ inches x 10 feet 3½ inches.

Plate 23. Peter Gui Clausen. *St. Anthony Falls: Break in the Tunnel*, No. 1, 1869. St. Paul.
Courtesy of Minnesota Historical Society. Oil on canvas, 15 x 24½ inches.

Plate 24. Alexander F. Loemans. *River Scene*, 1877. Minneapolis. Collection of the author. Oil on canvas, 21¾ x 36⅛ inches.

Plate 25. Herbjørn Gausta. *Setting the Trap*, 1908. Decorah, Ia. Courtesy
of Norwegian-American Museum. Luther College Collection.
Oil on canvas, 20½ x 25¾ inches.

Plate 26. Anton Gág, Ignatz Schwendinger, Christian Heller. *Cherub Panel*, 1892.
New Ulm. Courtesy of City Museum and Brown County Historical Society.
Oil on plaster plaque, 22 x 60 inches.

Plate 27. Anton Gág, Ignatz Schwendinger, Christian Heller. *Cherub Panel*, 1892.
New Ulm. Courtesy of City Museum and Brown County Historical Society.
Oil on plaster plaque, 22 x 60 inches.

Plate 28. Nicholas R. Brewer. *Landscape of River's Edge*. St. Paul. Private
collection. Oil on canvas, 14¼ x 17¼ inches.

Plate 29. Elijah E. Edwards. *The Devil's Chair*, 1880's. Private collection. Oil on canvas, 18¾ x 12¾ inches.

Plate 30. Thomas Cantwell Healy. *Portrait of Henry H. Sibley*, 1860. St. Paul. Courtesy of Minnesota Historical Society. Oil on canvas, 30 x 25 inches.

Plate 31. Douglas Volk. *Interior with Portrait of John Scott Bradstreet*. Minneapolis.
Courtesy of The Minneapolis Institute of Arts. Gift of Mr. John Scott Bradstreet.
Oil on canvas, 17 x 22¼ inches.

Plate 32. Robert Koehler. *The Strike*, 1886. New York. Collection of
Lee Raymond Baxandall. Oil on canvas, 78 x 110 inches.

Plate 33. Robert Koehler. *Rainy Evening on Hennepin Avenue*, c. 1910. Minneapolis.
Courtesy of The Minneapolis Institute of Arts. The Koehler Fund.
Oil on canvas, 25¾ x 24 inches.

Plate 34. Alexander Grinager. *Boys Bathing*, 1894. Minneapolis. Courtesy of The
Minneapolis Institute of Arts. Gift of Mr. and Mrs. Alex Grinager.
Oil on canvas, 34 x 59 inches.

Plate 35. Alexis Jean Fournier. *Ft. Snelling*, 1888. St. Paul. Courtesy of Minnesota Historical Society. Oil on canvas, 53 x 106 inches.

Plate 36. Alexis Jean Fournier. *Mill Pond at Minneapolis,* 1888. Minneapolis. Courtesy of The Minneapolis Institute of Arts. The John R. Van Derlip Fund. Oil on canvas, 17 x 26 inches.

Plate 37. Alexis Jean Fournier. *Lake Harriet by Moonlight*, 1889. Minneapolis. Courtesy
of Hennepin County Historical Society. Oil on canvas, 30⅛ x 40¼ inches.

hospitable to the practice of art by professionals, and even a painter of established reputation, like Charles Noel Flagg (1848–1916), found it hard going. Flagg was a friend of Frank Bass, whom he had known when they were students together in Paris, and through his friend's urging, he established residence in St. Paul in the late 1880's. Although he did receive a number of portrait commissions, his unsuccessful attempts to revive the idea of establishing an art school discouraged him enough so that he returned to New York, where his talents were better appreciated. Gilbert Davis Munger (1837–1903) also lived in Minnesota, briefly in 1867 and for more extensive periods in the 1870's. He painted Minnehaha Falls and other Minnesota scenes, including an 1871 view of Duluth (fig. 57). For a while he traveled in the Far West in the company of Albert Bierstadt, but in 1876 he moved to London, where he received commissions to paint pictures of American scenery, which were extravagantly praised. Success followed him to France, where he was overwhelmed by the softly glowing landscapes of the French Barbizon School. Thenceforth he adopted the Barbizon style as his own. When he returned to America, he established a studio in New York but, in failing health, moved a few years later to the milder climate of Washington, D.C. He died there on January 27, 1903.

Though Munger's reputation was made outside of Minnesota, there were, despite the hardships, some who became successful "Minnesota artists." One of these was the Danish-born Peter Gui Clausen (1830–1924), who had studied at the Royal academies of both Copenhagen and Stockholm. He had painted church frescoes, stage curtains, and ornamental pictures. But in spite of Peter's promising career, the defeat of Denmark by Germany and Austria in a struggle over the provinces of Schleswig and Holstein induced the Clausen family to emigrate to America in 1866. They settled first in Chicago, but in 1867 Peter came to Minneapolis to paint frescoes in the recently completed Universalist Church of the Redeemer. He returned two years later, took up permanent residence in Minneapolis, and remained a citizen of the state until his death in 1924.

Clausen not only painted church frescoes, landscapes, and portraits but, perhaps even more important for the progress of art in the area, gave art lessons in Minneapolis for a period of almost thirty years. It is interesting that he painted scenery and drop curtains for many of the theaters and auditoriums throughout Minnesota, because, probably as an offshoot of that, he painted a panorama too. Perhaps he lacked the necessary flamboyant showmanship, for it did not bring him much in the way of financial reward. Clausen's panorama, which occupied him from 1884 to 1888 was a small one measured by Banvard's standards. Eight feet high by eight hundred feet wide, its one hundred scenes depicted the West from Minneapolis's Lake Harriet to Mount Rainier in the state of Washington with North Dakota farms, gold mines, lumber camps, and Yellowstone National Park along the way. For a while the artist traveled with his panorama through the Middle West and eastern states. Disaster struck, however, for a fire in the Brooklyn theater where it was being shown destroyed it. The panorama was uninsured and financed by Clausen's mortgaged home. Discouraged and dispirited, the artist returned to Minneapolis and started over again, painting frescoes, landscapes, and portraits for the rest of his long life.

Though the panorama and much of Clausen's other work has disappeared, enough examples remain to give an indication of his style. One of these, *Minnehaha Falls* (fig. 58), though small, has something of the stage designer's feeling for generalized statement and simple forms and colors. It depicts the rough wooden bridge which once spanned the stream beneath the falls and a gentleman and lady who are walking up the steep path to enjoy a closer look at Minneapolis's famous landmark. Three other Clausen paintings (figs. 59, 60, and plate 23) depict the Falls of St. Anthony and were painted in 1869, the first year of the artist's permanent residence in Minnesota. A newspaper reporter interviewing the artist many years later quoted him as saying that when he first came to Minnesota and saw the great Mississippi he was "surprised to see anything so grand," even though he had been greatly impressed by pictures of the Mississippi

Fig. 57. Gilbert Munger. *View of Duluth*, 1871. Duluth. Courtesy of Duluth Public Library.
Oil on canvas, 24¾ x 49⅞ inches.

that he had seen in Denmark.[1] When he returned to Minneapolis in 1869, he was disappointed that he had not painted the power of the untamed river on his previous visit, for now workmen were cutting away the soft rocks and diverting the water away from the falls. Nevertheless, he found a rocky perch in the river and set about immediately to capture the river's strength as it was being brought under control to serve the new communities on its banks. Thus, he depicted the jumble of broken boulders, the spill of water, the buildings on either side, and the old high wooden bridge in precise and realistic detail. Using a cool color scheme and a linear style, Clausen emphasizes narrative rather than purely painterly values, for Clausen's purpose was to describe his environment rather than to manipulate it for abstract artistic ends. *Break in the Tunnel* (plate 23), showing the view upriver after a tunnel under the falls collapsed, provides

an especially vivid glimpse of the frontier communities of Minneapolis and St. Anthony over a hundred years ago.

Alexander F. Loemans (active 1864–1894), a St. Anthony artist who was much admired in his own day, was more inclined to romanticize his surroundings than Clausen. The facts of his life are sketchily known. Apparently born in France, or of French parentage, he was in Delaware County, New York, in 1864, when he painted a landscape of Eddy's Gap. He subsequently traveled west, for from 1873 to 1880 the Minneapolis city directories list him as "artist" and "landscape painter" residing at an address in St. Anthony. He was known for his scenic views of the area, including Minnehaha Falls, Fort Snelling, and views of St. Anthony based on old settlers' memories of it in earlier days. His method was probably the one current at the time—sketching a scene out-of-doors and then

Fig. 58. Peter Gui Clausen. *Minnehaha Falls*. St. Paul. Private collection.
Oil on canvas, 16⅛ x 12½ inches.

Fig. 59. Peter Gui Clausen. *St. Anthony Falls, Break in the Tunnel*, No. 2, 1869.
St. Paul. Courtesy of Minnesota Historical Society. Oil on canvas, 15 x 24½ inches.

actually painting it in the studio according to certain academic conventions. *River Scene* (plate 24), painted in 1877, is one such "studio piece." It depicts a Minnesota stream on a hot and sultry summer afternoon when the quiet surface of the water is disturbed only by a few floating lily pads. On either side the lush and shadowy riverbanks suggest a remote wilderness area far from the noise and activity of city life. The sky is filled with high-piled clouds edged with light and touched at the far left with rainbow colors. They suggest a rain shower that has just washed the near countryside but that still hovers in the darker distance. The careful realism combined with an ideali-

zation of nature, the richness of detail, even the heavy atmosphere all suggest the artist's exposure to the landscapes of the Düsseldorf tradition and his adherence to its painting formulas. In further search of the romantic scene, Loemans apparently left Minnesota around 1880 for more remote frontiers, though for some years his family continued to reside at the St. Anthony address. In the 1880's and 1890's he was living in Canada, and, drawn to the most dramatic aspects of nature, he painted the Sierra Nevada and the Canadian Rockies. Loemans even traveled to South America, for he painted scenes of the Andes in a style that is reminiscent of Frederic E. Church, though it is

Fig. 60. Peter Gui Clausen. *St. Anthony Falls, Nicollet Island Bridge*, 1869. St. Paul.
Courtesy of Minnesota Historical Society. Oil on canvas, 15 x 24½ inches.

drier, tighter, and less consciously pictureque. In the early 1890's he was living in Vancouver, British Columbia, where he died in 1894.

James Deverreux Larpenteur (1847–c. 1915) was also a well known artist in the Twin Cities during the 1880's. His 1886 pen and ink drawing of an old log house at the corner of Snelling and St. Anthony avenues (fig. 61) reveals the confident stroke of the trained artist. Larpenteur had, in fact, gone to Paris in 1867 and, after a number of years of study and travel there, returned to St. Paul in 1883. He specialized in pictures of European landscapes, though the local scene did, occasionally, catch his eye. His draw-

ing of a log cabin built in 1846 is almost a documentary representation of a rough pioneer homestead. The rain barrels and lean-to shed, the dogs and scratching chickens in the front yard, all describe a life that was simple, hard-working, and close to the soil.

Though there were, undoubtedly, other painters in the Twin Cities area in the 1870's and 1880's, few of their canvases survive. Outside of the urban area, however, artists were beginning to appear among the immigrant settlers on Minnesota's farmlands. Prominent among them was Herbjørn Gausta (1854–1924), the first professional painter of real ability of Norwegian-American origin.[2] Born in Telemark, Norway, he

Fig. 61. James Deverreux Larpenteur. *Log House in Rose Township*, 1886. St. Paul.
Courtesy of Minnesota Historical Society. Pen and ink drawing, 7 x 12 inches.

immigrated with his family to a farm near Harmony, Minnesota, in 1867. When his father died two years later, the family, in which Herbjørn was the only son, found itself in straitened circumstances. Nevertheless, Herbjørn managed to complete a three-year course of study at Luther College in Decorah, Iowa. Through the assistance of friends there, he was then sent abroad to study art in Oslo and Munich from 1874 to 1881. In 1888, after several restless *Wanderjahre*, he settled in Minneapolis, where he lived until his death in 1924.

One of the first pictures that Gausta painted after his return from Europe is *The Lay Preacher* of 1884 (fig. 62). Though based on an earlier interpretation of this theme in the romantic Düsseldorf manner by the Norwegian painter Adolf Tidemand,[3] Gausta's

work reveals the more modern realism of the Munich Academy, which he attended from 1878 to 1882 and where he won the Academy Medal in 1881. During the 1870's and 1880's Munich was succeeding in challenging even the supremacy of Paris as a mecca for art students. The established ateliers of the French capital, with their insistence on a romantic idealism couched in neoclassic terms, had begun to lose some of their following. As a newspaper article of 1882 explained it, "Mr. Gausta belongs to the newer so-called 'realistic' school of painting. As opposed to romanticism . . . which tried to 'beautify' nature, the realistic school makes an object of giving us nature as it is."[4]

Gausta's *The Lay Preacher* with its loose and vigorous brushwork, its dark tones and strong highlights,

Fig. 62. Herbjørn Gausta. *The Lay Preacher*, 1884. Decorah, Ia. Courtesy of Norwegian-
American Museum. Luther College Collection. Oil on canvas, 18 x 24 inches.

Fig. 63. Herbjørn Gausta. *Portrait of the
Rev. H. A. Stub*, 1886. Decorah, Ia. Courtesy of
Norwegian-American Museum. Luther College
Collection. Oil on canvas, 26¾ x 21½ inches.

and, above all, its rough, unidealized portraits does indeed give us nature as it is. It also, however, reveals the artist's familiarity with the contemporary French painters Manet and Degas.[5] Their off-center compositions and frequently oblique views into the picture plane reflected, in turn, the similar composition of Japanese prints then enjoying a considerable vogue in the Parisian art world. Gausta's moralistic subject matter sets it apart, however, from the more casual themes usually chosen by the French painters.

The strong modeling and direct observation shown in the representation of the portraits of the preacher and his small congregation are also revealed in Gausta's fine individual portraits. Those executed in 1886 of the Reverend and Mrs. H. A. Stub (figs. 63 and 64), for instance, though painted more tightly and with a harder edge, still afford us a penetrating glimpse into the personalities of the sitters and convey that sense of immediate presence which we call a "speaking likeness."

In a later painting, *Setting the Trap*, done in 1908 (plate 25), Gausta returned to the off-center composition of *The Lay Preacher*. Here he employed an even looser brush technique in which the quality of the paint itself and the tangible evidence of its application on the canvas provide the picture's richness of texture. It is a fresh and appealing composition, whose child subject, sunny light, and low vantage point that entirely dismisses a horizon line relate it to the French Impressionists—whose work Gausta may well have seen on his several trips to Europe. The picture is, in fact, a gleam of light in the declining artistic vitality of Gausta's later years.

The immigrant German and Austrian communities, as well as the Scandinavian one, produced artists who dreamed of following their profession in the midst of the farms of south central Minnesota. In New Ulm three men, Anton Gág, Ignatz Schwendinger, and Christian Heller, opened an art school in 1892 on the main street of the town. They decorated the school's three rooms with murals (really oil on plaster plaques) depicting cherubs with fruit and flower garlands (plates 26 and 27), in a brave attempt at transplanting the traditions of European rococo painting to rural Minnesota. The school lasted only a few months, but it is important as the first serious effort to make art a profession outside of Minnesota's metropolitan areas.

Anton Gág (1859–1908), the most accomplished of the three, settled in New Ulm in 1872 in an Old World environment created there by German, Bohemian, Bavarian, and Swiss immigrants. The oldest of his seven children was Wanda Gág, an even better known painter and illustrator whose productive life lies beyond the scope of this book. Anton supported his family, meagerly, by decorating churches and even painting houses in New Ulm. As his sensitive and well-modeled *Self-Portrait* (fig. 65) shows, however, he was capable of better things, and on Sundays he would retire to his attic studio to produce "real" art and to indulge in the one cigar he allowed himself each week. He had studied briefly, as a young immigrant, at the art schools of Milwaukee and Chicago, and he nourished a forlorn hope of returning to Europe some day to study painting there. Meanwhile, he continued to paint houses and decorate churches; and, having learned to use the camera, he opened New Ulm's first commercial photography studio. In 1892–1893 Gág painted a panorama of the New Ulm massacre (figs. 66 and 67), incorporating eleven panels which depict the Sioux uprising of 1862. A separate painting also exists by Gág of the battle between New Ulm farmers and the desperate and starving Indians. In this dark chapter of Minnesota history, the Sioux, under Chief Little Crow, rose up against white encroachment on Indian lands, against treaties of questionable integrity that they had been tricked into signing, and against unfulfilled promises of food and protection. Gág's panorama reveals the narrative style of an accomplished artist attempting to describe with pictorial accuracy the events of the summer of 1862. The figures exist in convincing space, the pioneer town and surrounding countryside are truthfully represented, and the action is clearly and correctly portrayed. If something of the melodrama of the stage scenery painter is also revealed here, it is still a painting that reflects the at-

Fig. 64. Herbjørn Gausta. *Portrait of Mrs. H. A. Stub*, 1886. Decorah, Ia. Courtesy of Norwegian-American Museum. Luther College Collection. Oil on canvas, 26¾ x 21½ inches.

Fig. 65. Anton Gág. *Self-Portrait*. Present whereabouts unknown. Oil on canvas.

titudes of Minnesota's white settlers as they pushed the Indians away from their ancestral lands.

The early history of the Gág panorama is not known, but it was discovered in 1955 in Poughkeepsie, New York, water stained and in poor condition. Purchased by the Minnesota Historical Society, it is in storage awaiting funds to conserve and restore it to such condition that it may be exhibited as a rare example of panorama painting and an important monument of the art of the early state.

Among Anton Gág's colleagues in New Ulm's small art community was an Austrian immigrant named Ignatz Schwendinger (1831–1904). As a youth he had studied painting, sculpture, and the new art of photography. In 1879 he came to America and settled in New Ulm, where he first earned his living as a stonecutter. There exist a number of small portraits in oil on zinc that he painted of the officers of a local brewing company and also a small wooden medallion, carved in 1882, of the Reverend Alex Berghold (fig. 68). All of them reveal the skill and knowledge of a trained, if provincial, artist. Ignatz's son Alex was associated with Gág in New Ulm's short-lived art school and worked with him on the cherub panels that decorated it. He also painted a number of large canvases including a representation of the New Ulm massacre, a picture of Christopher Columbus on the *Santa María*, and copies of old master paintings.

Rochester and its environs, though not as artistically active as New Ulm in its early days, nevertheless was the home of a number of men who became professional painters. John Stevens (1816–1879), for example, whose panorama of the Sioux uprising has already been described in chapter III, settled in Rochester as early as 1855. He was a sign and house painter by trade, and his first painted work in the area was the decoration of the bandwagon that carried the Rochester Brass Band to neighboring towns. During the 1860's he was occupied in producing and displaying his panoramas, but in the 1870's he settled on a farm in Dodge County and devoted himself to portrait

Fig. 66.
Anton Gág. *New Ulm Massacre:
Flight from New Ulm to Mankato.*
Panorama detail, 1892–1893. St. Paul.
Courtesy of Minnesota Historical
Society. 7 x 10 feet.

Fig. 67.
Anton Gág. *New Ulm Massacre:
Second Battle of New Ulm.* Panorama
detail, 1892–1893. St. Paul.
Courtesy of Minnesota Historical
Society. 7 x 10 feet.

painting. His *Self-Portrait* (fig. 69) reveals the same stiff modeling and hard contours of the panorama figures but monumentalized here in a careful portrait. Though it may lack the psychological penetration of Herbjørn Gausta's portraits of Reverend and Mrs. Stub, it nevertheless presents a clear image of Rochester's painter-showman.

Another Olmsted County artist who eventually made a reputation as a much sought-after painter was Nicholas R. Brewer (1857–1949), who was born to pioneer parents on a farm near High Forest, Minnesota. The painting entitled *Landscape, River Scene* (fig. 70) is a youthful effort, painted when he was only sixteen and, at that time, entirely self-taught. It reveals the typical bright colors and stock figures of the primitive painter and the same sense of earnest endeavor, but it was enough to persuade his family and friends that he was destined for a great artistic career. His father could not afford to pay his expenses at an art school, but he managed to start him off with a load of wheat —forty bushels—which Nicholas and his brother hauled to Rochester. With the thirty-four dollars from the sale of the wheat, Nicholas boarded a train for St. Paul, where he received his first art lessons from one Henry J. Koempel, a history painter from Cincinnati, whose daughter, Rose, became Brewer's wife. Eventually he was able to study in New York under Dwight William Tryon and Charles Noel Flagg. He returned to St. Paul and later became a successul portraitist and landscape painter. His early life and artistic career are entertainingly described in his autobiography, *Trails of a Paintbrush* (Boston, 1938).

A late but undated landscape by Brewer (plate 28) forms an interesting contrast to his primitive early work. It shows the influence of Tryon and other Americans whose style reflected Barbizon aesthetics. Like his teacher, Brewer now evokes, with a broad, sure stroke, the placid stillness of a country scene. There is little emphasis on a specific site, and the misty quiet is emphasized by the absence of man and beast. The harshness of Brewer's earlier palette has disappeared in favor of the muted tones and mellow atmosphere of the more sophisticated artist. This painting shares

Fig. 68. Ignatz Schwendinger. *Portrait of the Rev. Alex Berghold*, 1882. New Ulm. Courtesy of City Museum and Brown County Historical Society. Wooden medallion, 3½ inches in diameter.

with so many American landscapes of the period an elegiac mood and a taste for the more fragile beauties of nature.

A similar fragility in tone and mood distinguishes the work of the Reverend Elijah E. Edwards (1831–1915) of Taylors Falls, whose pictures, unlike Brewer's, specifically define their locale. Edwards was a man of many talents: clergyman, professor, writer, and principal of the Chisago Seminary. He was an artist as well, for whom the St. Croix River with its steep and rocky banks provided an endless source of inspiration and delight. "I have been a wanderer on the face of the earth," Edwards wrote in 1896, "but have not found any landscape rivaling the one shut in amongst [our] own green hills. It is a combination of that which is loveliest in many landscapes."[6] *The Gorge of the St. Croix* (fig. 71) is typical of Edwards's work. Painted in a thin oil wash in subdued tones of brown and gray, it reflects in its silent depths the quiet peace of a wilderness stream. Like *The Devil's Chair* (plate 29) illustrating one of the many fantastic rock formations of the St. Croix River, it was painted during the 1880's after Edwards had returned to Taylors Falls from a residence of some years in Colorado and Missouri. His paintings, together with his frequent articles and lectures, helped to arouse enough interest in the dells area to preserve it in its natural state. By their suggestion of the eternity of nature in her elemental forms of rock, water, and sky and by the absence of man, whose transience is thus made implicit, Edwards's paintings become provincial reflections of the eastern seaboard's Hudson River School.

Among his many activities, Elijah Edwards managed to find time to give instruction in art as well. One of his pupils was Harriet Lee Gwynne (d. 1899), some of whose landscapes and flower pictures survive in the Taylors Falls area. They are typical of the numerous pleasant paintings, some of them quite accomplished, done by women whose lives, bound by the duties of home and family, precluded the serious pursuit of art.

May Roos (c. 1871–1961), also of Taylors Falls, was one of the few exceptions. She was the daughter of

Fig. 69. John Stevens. *Self-Portrait*, c. 1880. Rochester. Courtesy of Olmsted County Historical Society. Photo-oil, 12 x 9 inches.

Fig. 70. Nicholas R. Brewer. *Landscape, River Scene*, c. 1873. Rochester. Courtesy of Olmsted County Historical Society. Oil on canvas, 11½ x 17⅝ inches.

Fig. 71. Elijah E. Edwards. *The Gorge of the St. Croix*. St. Paul. Courtesy of
Minnesota Historical Society. Oil on canvas, 17 x 28 inches.

Fig. 72. May Roos. *Self-Portrait*, 1893.
Private collection. Oil on
canvas, 12 x 9¼ inches.

Oscar Roos (1827–1896), the first painter among the Swedish immigrants to Minnesota and therefore a person who could be expected to encourage the development of artistic talent among his children. May studied painting with the Sisters of St. Joseph at St. Agatha's Conservatory of Music and Art in St. Paul in the 1880's. For her, painting was a professional occupation, and she devoted herself to it with industry and dedication. Her small *Self-Portrait* (fig. 72), painted in 1893, combines confidence with delicacy in a charming and accomplished portrait of the young artist at the beginning of her career.

Duluth, too, had a number of artists struggling to succeed in their profession in an environment that did not always reward their efforts. One of these was Peter F. Lund (d. 1902), a Norwegian immigrant about whom not very much is known. It is thought that early in life he was a sailor. Apparently his love of the sea never left him, for he later specialized in "marine views," many of which were painted along the north shore of Lake Superior (fig. 73). In the late 1880's and early 1890's he made his home first in Minneapolis and then in Duluth at which time he painted *Logging Camp in Winter* (fig. 74). In a loose, rather sketchy style, he depicted the snowy clearing in the north woods, the rough log bunk houses that shelter the lumberjacks, and the surrounding pine forest. In spite of some awkwardness, it is a direct and unembellished view of a typical northern Minnesota scene—far from the tight realism and romantic idealization of the Düsseldorf school. His brushwork reveals enough dexterity to indicate some academic training, but whether in America or in Europe is not known. Lund left Minnesota some time during the 1890's and moved to New York. Since he exhibited a painting entitled *Moonlight on Lake Superior* at the National Academy of Design in November and December of 1897, he seems to have won, by then, full acceptance by the established art community.

A similar view of northern Minnesota was painted the same year, 1889, as Lund's *Logging Camp in Winter* by an even more obscure artist named William A. Sussmilch, who is listed in Duluth's city directories

Fig. 73. Peter Lund. *North Shore of Lake Superior*, c. 1890. Minneapolis. Courtesy of The Minneapolis Institute of Arts. Oil on canvas, 22 x 36 inches.

Fig. 74. Peter Lund. *Logging Camp in Winter*, 1889. Duluth. Courtesy of St. Louis County Historical Society. Oil on canvas, 17 x 27⅛ inches.

simply as "artist." His painting of a logging scene in Minnesota (fig. 75) has the same straightforward observation of nature as Lund's, the same loose brushwork, and the same ability to evoke the quality of a typical winter's day in the north woods. Sussmilch, however, was more interested than Lund in the lumberman himself. He portrayed him, tall and stalwart, beside the log-piled sled and the plodding team of oxen hauling it. Sussmilch's lumberman is suggestive

of the legendary hero of Minnesota's logging industry, Paul Bunyan.

The importance of the logging industry to Minnesota is, in fact, underscored by the number of times it was the subject of an artist's brush. Still another logging enterprise was recorded in 1892 in *Logging Scene* (fig. 76) by Feodor von Luerzer. Von Luerzer was an Austrian-born artist who lived in Duluth from 1889 to 1909. His style is essentially a painterly one,

Fig. 75. William A. Sussmilch. *Logging Scene in Minnesota*, 1889. Duluth. Courtesy of
St. Louis County Historical Society. Oil on canvas, 10 x 16¼ inches.

with the brush moving rapidly over the canvas and the paint itself catching the light and creating a sketchy but nonetheless vivid impression of a northern Minnesota landscape. These qualities are even more evident in the artist's *Autumn Landscape with Pond* (fig. 77), which was also, in all likelihood, from his Duluth period.

The landscapes of these artists—even the several logging scenes discussed here—are provincial counter-parts of the pastoral landscapes of the French Barbizon School of a generation or so earlier. There is the same quiet but direct observation of nature, the same poetic interpretation of its manifold moods, and above all, the same view of man, whether French peasant or Minnesota lumberjack, as an integral and occasionally monumental part of the natural scene.

Among the artist-settlers, as among artists elsewhere, though landscapes might frequently have been their

Fig. 76. Feodor von Luerzer. *Logging Scene*, 1892. Duluth. Courtesy of St. Louis County Historical Society. Oil on canvas, 17⅞ x 24 inches.

Fig. 77. Feodor von Luerzer. *Autumn Landscape with Pond*. Duluth. Courtesy of St. Louis County Historical Society. Oil on canvas, 15⅛ x 23⅜ inches.

preference, portraits were their steadiest source of income and, therefore, their bread and butter. Occasionally the two would be combined and the sitter would be portrayed in an idealized landscape setting. It is rare, however, to find portraiture combined with marine views, and the painting of the steamer *Manistee* (fig. 78) by Herbert L. Conner (1851–1933)[7] is, therefore, particularly interesting in this respect. It shows the ship's captain and chief engineer framed in medallions similar to portrait miniatures, which are suspended by delicate chains from the top of the picture.[8] The *Manistee* plows bravely through the heavy waters of the lake under a low and threatening sky, but also under the protective shelter, as it were, of its two guardian angels. Their protection had proven inadequate, however. On November 15, 1883, heavily laden with cargo, the *Manistee* had run into one of Lake Superior's treacherous late fall storms. The ship foundered in the heavy seas and sank with all its passengers and crew beneath the cold dark waters of the lake. Perhaps the painting was intended as a memorial to the *Manistee* and all aboard her on her last, fateful voyage.

Usually, however, portraits are not part of the stuff of melodrama. Most of them are quiet studies that attempt to reveal the personality of the sitter while glossing over his (or her) less favorable features. Few reach the psychological penetration of the portraits by Herbjørn Gausta, discussed above, but they range, in great numbers, from the primitive to the most accomplished. *Self-Portrait* by John Banvard (fig. 17), for example, is a competent and professional representation. It shows the artist-showman of the three-mile panorama as an alert and rather delicate-featured young man. The pair of portraits of Mr. and Mrs. Burleigh Smart (figs. 79 and 80) by an anonymous artist are painted with a harder line, a tighter realism, and, one suspects, a good deal less flattery. In fact, the unembellished candor of the portrait of Mrs. Smart relates it to the tradition of American primitive portraiture. But the portraits of Mr. and Mrs. Henry Rice (figs. 81 and 82), painted in 1861 by George Peter Alexander Healy, are done in the best academic tradition of their day. Healy (1813–1894) was one of the most successful portrait painters in America in the nineteenth century and one of the century's most enthusiastic name droppers.[9] He began his artistic career in his native Boston and in 1834, at the age of seventeen, went to Paris to study under the well-known French painter Baron Antoine Jean Gros. When he returned to America eight years later, he had an established international reputation which included the patronage of many of the crowned heads of Europe. In the United States, too, he received innumerable portrait commissions from some of the most prominent American statesmen of the day. From 1854 to 1867 he made his home in Chicago, and it was during this period that the Rice portraits were painted.

Though George P. A. Healy can scarcely be considered a Minnesota settler,[10] his sitter, Henry M. Rice, was prominent in the history of the state from the time of his first arrival at Fort Snelling in 1839 as an alert and ambitious twenty-one-year-old youth. Vermont-born and with some education in the law, he soon made a name for himself in the business and politics of the new state. He was active in trade with the Winnebago, became a partner in John Jacob Astor's American Fur Company, and in 1857 was elected one of the first two senators from Minnesota to the national Congress in Washington. It was probably there, in fact, in 1861, that the two portraits of Senator and Mrs. Rice were painted.

The portraits reveal the skillful modeling, the effective use of tone, and the facile ability to capture a flattering likeness that undoubtedly accounted for Healy's enormous popularity. His brush eloquently portrays Henry Rice as a serious and purposeful man of state, and his wife as an attractive and stylish lady—surely the way each wished to be memorialized in the cultural atmosphere of mid-nineteenth-century America.

Rice's close business and political associate—and occasional rival as well—was Henry H. Sibley, Minnesota's first governor. Sibley's portrait (plate 30) was painted in 1860 by Thomas Cantwell Healy (1820–1873), the younger brother of George P. A. Healy.

Fig. 78. Herbert L. Conner. S.S. *Manistee*, 1897. Duluth. Courtesy of St. Louis
County Historical Society. Oil on canvas, 23¾ x 35¾ inches.

Fig. 79. Anon. *Portrait of Burleigh Smart.*
St. Paul. Courtesy of Minnesota Historical Society.
Oil on canvas, 30 x 25 inches.

Fig. 80. Anon. *Portrait of Abigail Cogswell Smart.*
St. Paul. Courtesy of Minnesota Historical Society.
Oil on canvas, 29 x 25 inches.

Thomas Healy was born in Albany, New York, grew up in Boston, and, like his brother, received his training in art in Paris. In the 1850's he visited his older brother, George, in Chicago, and in 1857 he spent some time in St. Paul, where he received a number of portrait commissions. He later established himself in Port Gibson, Mississippi, where he lived through the Civil War and possibly on until his death in 1873. Though not quite as successful as his brother, he apparently made a good enough living painting such portraits as Sibley's, which are executed in a tight, rather dry style that concentrates on surface realism but does not probe too deeply into the essential character or personality of the sitter.

It was not always the rich and famous, the notable statemen and the captains of industry, who sat for their portraits. More humble people were also portrayed, though more frequently by primitive artists than by professional ones. Still, even professional artists were drawn to colorful local "types," those whose lives or backgrounds would add intrinsic drama to their portraits. This is the case in the portrait of "Uncle Jim" Carter (fig. 83), painted about 1900 by Mrs. Sadie Stephens Clark of Stillwater. Mrs. Clark (d.

Fig. 81. George Peter Alexander Healy. *Portrait of Mr. Henry Rice*, 1861. St. Paul. Courtesy of Minnesota Historical Society. Oil on canvas, 30 x 25 inches.

Fig. 82. George Peter Alexander Healy. *Portrait of Mrs. Henry Rice*, 1861. St. Paul. Courtesy of Minnesota Historical Society. Oil on canvas, 30 x 25 inches.

1899), the wife of a Stillwater physician, may be considered an amateur artist in the sense that her painting was an avocation rather than her bread and butter, but she can scarcely be called a primitive one. Her portrait of the black man who was, for many years, Stillwater's odd-jobs man and hack driver is a skillful as well as sympathetic portrayal. Unlike the primitive painting which generally relies on flat pattern and decorative line for effect, even in portraits, Mrs. Clark's "Uncle Jim" is realized in true three-dimensional perspective. His head and shoulders emerge convincingly from the picture space as they

are built up in layers of tone and color by the artist's broad brushstrokes. The portrait manages, moreover, to subtly capture the patience and sadness of a rather lonely man.

The same type of local character is portrayed in *Old Bets* (fig. 84), the portrait of an old Sioux woman from Shakopee, painted about 1870 by Dr. Andrew Falkenshield. Falkenshield (1822?–1896) was an immigrant from Denmark who had been a surgeon in the Danish army during the Schleswig-Holstein war. Some time during the 1850's he came to New York City, where he continued to practice medicine but also took up drawing and painting as a hobby. After a few years there, he moved west, first to Chicago, where he gave up medicine for art, and then, in 1856, to St. Paul. There he opened up a gallery and, apparently, gave instruction in art as well. One of his pupils was Elijah Edwards, who studied oil painting with him during the winter of 1863–1864, apparently Edwards's only formal training in art. Falkenshield also took up photography, and it is possible that the portrait of Old Bets was painted over a photograph, a technique not uncommon at the time. Like "Uncle Jim" Carter in his portrait, Old Bets regards the observer with that characteristic mixture of resignation and dignity that is typical of nineteenth-century images of Indians and blacks. One can trace such images, in fact, all the way back to the portraits of Tishcohan and Lapowinsa, painted in 1735 by the Maryland artist Gustavus Hesselius. These two formerly powerful chiefs of the Leni Lenape nation became, in fact, paradigms for the portrayal of the American Indian accepting in weary defeat the triumph of an alien civilization. In the portrait of Old Bets, however, force of personality, as expressed in the image of the old woman, seems to triumph over defeat.

Sculpture was an art that was practiced more rarely than painting in Minnesota—or elsewhere in the United States—in the last century. As already mentioned, it is an expensive medium and one that is a good deal less portable than painting. It therefore depends on a well-established community and generous private or civic commissions in order to flourish. Moreover, the iconoclastic attitudes of Puritan America, its opposition to "graven images," undoubtedly did much to inhibit this particular art form. In spite of all this, however, some sculpture did exist. Woodcarving by primitive artists, Lars Christenson notable among them, was occasionally practiced, usually with a religious purpose in mind. Thus, Peter Winnen and S. Dietel are mentioned in the St. Paul press, the former in 1864 for having carved an ornamental headboard for a grave and the latter in 1875 for the carved figures of saints he made for local churches. Marble sculpture was even more rare, though in 1866 Robert Powie exhibited a bust of Ulysses S. Grant at the Rochester

Fig. 83. Sadie Stephens Clark. *Portrait of "Uncle Jim" Carter,* c. 1900. Stillwater. Courtesy of Washington County Historical Society. Oil on canvas, 18¼ x 22 inches.

Fig. 84. Dr. Andrew Falkenshield. *Portrait of Old Bets*, c. 1870. St. Paul. Courtesy of
Minnesota Historical Society. Photo-oil(?), 16 x 14 inches.

fair. In 1887, however, Jacob H. F. Fjelde arrived in Minneapolis, and with him sculpture became part of the art produced in and for Minnesota.

It is significant, in the light of what has already been said about the history of sculpture in Minnesota, that Jacob Fjelde (1855–1896) started off his career as a woodcarver in his native Norway, thus inheriting the same tradition of fine wood craftsmanship out of which Minnesota's primitive sculptors emerged. But Fjelde had ambitions that went far beyond carving wood in his spare time, and he enrolled as a student of sculpture in the Royal Academy of Art in Copenhagen. For a short time after that he lived and worked in Rome, then the mecca of all aspiring young sculptors. Undoubtedly, he came under the influence there of the smooth neoclassic sculpture of Antonio Canova and his Danish disciple, Bertel Thorwaldsen. In 1887 Fjelde immigrated to the United States and settled in Minneapolis, where he lived until his early death at the age of forty-one.

As the only resident sculptor with both ability and academic credentials, Fjelde had little difficulty in obtaining commissions for portraits of prominent Minnesotans. He also received civic commissions which resulted in well-known landmarks in both Minneapolis and St. Paul. One of these is the life-size bronze figure of the Scandinavian violinist Ole Bull in Loring Park. Another is the bust in Como Park of the great Norwegian dramatist Henrik Ibsen, Fjelde's countryman. Perhaps the best known, however, is the group of Minnehaha and Hiawatha in Minnehaha Park, the sculptor's model for which appears in figure 85. Inspired, as many before him had been, by Longfellow's poem, Fjelde represented the young lovers as European heroes based on vaguely classical prototypes and with little reference to their Indian nationality, either in facial features or even in dress. They are, instead, embodiments of that curious nineteenth-century attitude that idealized the Indian, in both literature and art, as a combination of Rousseau's "noble savage" and the stoic hero of classical mythology. This attitude persisted in American art until the end of the nineteenth century and the birth of the American cowboy as the new romantic hero of the West.

Fig. 85. Jacob Fjelde. Sculptor's model for *Minnehaha and Hiawatha Group* in Minnehaha Park. Minneapolis. Courtesy of Hennepin County Historical Society. Plaster, approx. 12 inches high.

VII The Capitol

Perhaps no other single event provided as strong an impetus to the development of art in Minnesota as the building of the State Capitol in St. Paul. It was designed and built by the St. Paul architect Cass Gilbert (1859–1934), who worked on the project from 1896, when ground was broken, to January, 1905, when the building was first occupied by the state legislature. Its architectural history lies outside the scope of this book, but the painting and sculpture with which it is decorated form an important chapter in the history of Minnesota art.

Gilbert, as both architect and project supervisor of the Capitol, envisioned a truly baroque blend of high-quality sculpture and painting to complement the architecture of his new building. Even before the first ground was turned, he had seen and admired Daniel Chester French's *The Triumph of Columbus*, a quadriga, or chariot group, which the Massachusetts sculptor had modeled for Chicago's World's Columbian Exposition of 1893. Daniel Chester French (1850–1931) was well known and much admired for his popular *Minute Man* statue in Concord, Massachusetts, and although he was Gilbert's second choice as sculptor (Augustus Saint-Gaudens was the unobtainable first choice), the architect approached French about a sculpture commission for the new building as early as the laying of the Capitol's cornerstone in

1896. Gilbert had in mind the placing of an allegorical quadriga representing the progress of the state (fig. 86) at the base of the Capitol's dome. This was in itself an innovation, for it departed from the usual practice of placing a classical pediment, or triangular member, above the main pavilion of such Renaissance revival façades as Gilbert had designed for the Capitol. He persisted and in 1903 the funds were finally appropriated and the sculpture contract signed. It called for a group containing "one chariot and human figure therein, four horses and two human figures attendant thereon" to be executed in copper and then gilded.[1] Collaborating on the project with French was Edward C. Potter (1857–1923), a noted sculptor of animals and equestrian statues.

The allegory of man's progress toward prosperity was typical both of the nineteenth century's optimism about the future and its tendency to monumentalize that optimism in classical personifications. Such allegories were thought to be particularly appropriate as freestanding sculpture or as applied reliefs for public buildings. The Capitol's quadriga shows Man in his triumphal chariot proceeding toward prosperity through the efforts of Nature, represented by the horses, and of Civilization, the "softening influence" represented by the women. To make allusion doubly clear, Man holds a horn of plenty in his right hand

93

and in his left a Roman standard inscribed "Minnesota" and festooned with garlands of native fruits and grains. In keeping with the sense of Roman splendor that the group was intended to evoke and in the interest of historical accuracy, the horses are even hitched to the chariot with the "choke" tugs of the ancient world rather than the "collar" harness of contemporary Minnesota.[2]

In addition to the quadriga French also made, in 1900, six allegorical figures in stone for the façade of the new Capitol. They are placed on the entablature above the second-story arcade and form a base, as it were, for the quadriga above. They, too, are allegorical and represent the civic and personal virtues of Truth, Bounty, Wisdom, Prudence, Courage, and Integrity. Like the chariot group their ultimate source is in the sculpture of the ancient classical world. But if the sculpture of the Capitol was not very original—and most American sculpture was essentially derivative until the revelations of Europe's avant-garde art in the New York Armory Show of 1913—it nevertheless displays great strength, grace, and energy. Moreover, in scale and design it is perfectly attuned to the noble dignity of the façade, and it satisfied the taste for grandeur demanded by the industrial barons and merchant princes of the time. Finally, the sculpture of the Capitol left a legacy of quality craftsmanship and careful attention to detail that was not the least contribution of Daniel Chester French to future generations of Minnesota sculptors.

For painters, too, the new Capitol in St. Paul provided the opportunity to compose monumental pictures of the history of the state and make allegorical references to its past or future virtues. In typical nineteenth-century fashion, the Board of County Commissioners, who, of course, controlled the purse strings, suggested as themes for the Capitol's murals illustrations of Minnesota's progress from wilderness to civilization, from empty prairie to settled cities and towns. On the whole, what they got was a series of paintings steeped in allegory and delivered with bombast. Because the sentiments the murals expressed were essentially artificial, they resulted in empty rhetoric on a

grand scale. There are, however, a few distinguished exceptions to the pervasive pedantry of the Capitol's murals, especially in the decoration of the Supreme Court Chamber, whose four lunettes, or architectural recesses, were painted by John La Farge (1835–1910) in 1904.

Though, like the others, La Farge's murals are allegorical, they do not illustrate clichés of progress but deal instead with four specific moments in history that illustrate advances in the relation between law and society. The first, which is positioned over the justices' bench, is entitled *The Moral and Divine Law* (fig. 87) and shows Moses receiving the law of God on Mount Sinai. The second, placed over the entrance to the chamber, is called *The Relation of the Moral Law to the State* (fig. 88) and deals with Socrates and Cephalus's discourse on the responsibilities of the artist to his subject and to his society.[3] *The Recording of Precedents* (fig. 89), to the left of the entrance, pictures Confucius seated in a Chinese garden with his disciples around him. The sage ponders the literature of the past in an allegory of the value of tradition to society. Finally, *The Adjustment of Conflicting Interests* (fig. 90), to the right of the chamber's entrance, depicts Count Raymond of Toulouse attempting to balance the conflicting claims of citizen, church, and state.

La Farge, the son of a cultivated New York family and Paris-trained, was already a well-known muralist and artist of many talents when he was asked to paint the St. Paul Capitol lunettes. He had behind him such well-received commissions as the mural and stained-glass decoration of Henry Hobson Richardson's monumental Trinity Church in Boston's Copley Square. Indeed, something of the luminous glow of the stained-glass medium appears in the St. Paul Capitol's lunettes. La Farge was, in fact, primarily a colorist who felt that, instead of the flat, cool effect desired by most contemporary muralists—including some of the other painters working in the Capitol—mural painting should describe form in rich, warm atmospheric color. The work itself was based on a large number of water-color sketches (such as the Socrates panel in

Fig. 86. Daniel Chester French. *Progress of the State*, c. 1905. Quadriga, Capitol. St. Paul.

Fig. 87. John La Farge. *The Moral and Divine Law*, 1903. Lunette, Supreme Court Chamber, Capitol. St. Paul. Oil on canvas.

Fig. 88. John La Farge. *The Relation of the Moral Law to the State*, 1903. Lunette, Supreme Court Chamber, Capitol. St. Paul. Oil on canvas.

Fig. 89. John La Farge. *The Recording of Precedents*, 1903. Lunette, Supreme Court
Chamber, Capitol. St. Paul. Oil on canvas.

Fig. 90. John La Farge. *The Adjustment of Conflicting Interests*, 1903. Lunette, Supreme
Court Chamber, Capitol. St. Paul. Oil on canvas.

Fig. 91. John La Farge. *The Relation of the Individual to the State*, 1903. New York.
Courtesy of Metropolitan Museum of Art. Bequest of Susan Dwight
Bliss, 1966. Water color, 9¾ x 11 inches.

figure 91), from which the designs were transferred to canvas. Assistants helped in the process because La Farge was subject to bouts of malaria and partially paralyzed by lead poisoning. But despite his illness, the final work was done by the artist himself. Though the murals were highly praised by contemporary critics, the fresher, more spontaneous quality of the water-color sketches with their rich and varied tones holds more appeal for modern audiences. It is a tribute to La Farge's ability, in fact, that he was able to retain a good deal of the glowing color of the water colors in such large *public* pictures as the Capitol's lunettes. Moreover, he was remarkably successful in choosing, out of his own cultural background, vivid images of classical, Oriental, medieval, and Renaissance history and in giving them both strength and dignity.

One other painter whose mural for the Minnesota State Capitol rose above insipid sentimentality was Kenyon Cox (1856–1919), who, like La Farge, was a well-known artist of his time and an art critic as well. His lunette, which is directly above the staircase leading to the Supreme Court Chamber, is entitled *The Contemplative Spirit of the East* (fig. 92). Here the artist has indulged in a bit of *trompe l'oeil*, or "fool-the-eye" painting, by continuing the yellowish color and texture of the real Kasota stone architrave into the two stone steps in the painting. Upon these steps are three massive allegorical figures. Thought, with violet blue feathered wings, sits in the center flanked by Law holding a bridle and Letters holding a book. Kenyon Cox's sculpturesque wall painting ultimately derives from Michelangelo's famous frescoes for the ceiling of the Sistine Chapel in Rome, which were admired and adapted by generations of artists of other eras and in such faraway places as St. Paul, Minnesota.

All the major murals executed for the Capitol were

not, in strict definition, murals at all, for they were not painted directly on the surface of the wall. They were, instead, painted on canvas in the artists' eastern studios and then shipped to St. Paul and permanently mounted in their appointed place. Six more pictures were originally commissioned as freestanding paintings, though they, too, are permanently installed within carved moldings in the governor's reception room. This room is a richly decorated chamber with white oak paneling, two huge marble fireplaces, and ornate plaster casts of regional fruits and seeds gilded with gold leaf. The artists who were commissioned to execute the paintings were specifically directed to illustrate six glorious events in the history of the state. They chose four scenes of Civil War battles, one of the Treaty of Traverse des Sioux, and one showing Father Louis Hennepin discovering the Falls of St. Anthony in 1680.

Douglas Volk (1856–1935) was the only local painter whose work was represented in the reception room. He was, in fact, the only Minnesota artist (besides the architect himself) to have been invited to do any work for the Capitol, for neither Cass Gilbert nor the Board of Capitol Commissioners seems to have made any effort to find and employ local talent. Volk's two Capitol paintings are *Father Hennepin Discovering the Falls of St. Anthony* (fig. 93) and *The Second Minnesota Regiment at the Battle of Mission Ridge* (fig. 94). The former picture shows the missionary-explorer holding up a cross and blessing the falls, while his companion, Picard du Gay, kneels in reverence at his feet and several Indians observe the ceremony with quiet interest. The Civil War picture depicts, with a more dramatic flourish, the Minnesota regiment charging up the ridge and ignoring enemy fire as the soldiers follow the intrepid example of their

Fig. 92. Kenyon Cox. *The Contemplative Spirit of the East.* Lunette, entrance to Supreme Court Chamber, Capitol, St. Paul. Oil on canvas.

Fig. 93. Douglas Volk. *Father Hennepin Discovering the Falls of St. Anthony.* Governor's
reception room, Capitol. St. Paul. Oil on canvas, 74 x 125 inches.

leader, Colonel J. W. Bishop. To achieve literal correctness the artist actually visited the battleground on the forty-second anniversary of the battle. The result is an amalgam of dry realism and self-conscious melodrama—a formula considered appropriate for *public* pictures. Fortunately, in Volk's smaller, more intimate paintings one finds a richness and warmth that better represent his artistic talents.

The best painting of the six in the governor's reception room is undoubtedly *Battle of Nashville* (fig. 95) by Howard Pyle (1853–1911). Pyle was one of the greatest illustrators in the history of American art and

a master, particularly, of the historical imagination. Though he, too, had a passion for antiquarian accuracy, he was able, in his many illustrations for children's stories and books on American history, to combine a love for the past with a fresh and vivid recreation of it. His stirring picture shows the Fifth, Seventh, Ninth, and Tenth Minnesota regiments arranged in a dark broken line against the slope of a barren hill. The masterly composition is enhanced by the warm glow of the setting sun shining through the smoke and haze of battle. The colors are luminous yet subdued, in keeping with the somberness of the sub-

Fig. 94. Douglas Volk. *The Second Minnesota Regiment at the Battle of Mission Ridge.*
Governor's reception room, Capitol. St. Paul. Oil on canvas, 74 x 96 inches.

Fig. 95. Howard Pyle. *Battle of Nashville*. Governor's reception room, Capitol.
St. Paul. Oil on canvas, 74 x 96 inches.

Fig. 96. Rufus Zogbaum. *Battle of Gettysburg.* Governor's reception room, Capitol. St. Paul. Oil on canvas, 74 x 96 inches.

Fig. 97. Francis D. Millet. *Fourth Minnesota Regiment Entering Vicksburg.* Governor's reception room, Capitol. St. Paul. Oil on canvas, 74 x 96 inches.

Fig. 98. Francis D. Millet. *Treaty of Traverse des Sioux*. Governor's reception room,
Capitol. St. Paul. Oil on canvas, 74 x 125 inches.

ject. Little pools of water in the foreground reflect the sky, for as Pyle made it his business to know, it had rained the morning of the battle. But such details, in Pyle's hands, are never obtrusive. They help to make the event come alive, as though the observer himself were there. Avoiding the tendency toward pedantry too often apparent in contemporary historical painting, Pyle was able to achieve the excitement and drama the others attempted but never quite achieved.

Typical of the latter was *Battle of Gettysburg* (fig. 96) by Rufus F. Zogbaum (1849–1925). He was a painter who was familiar with military and naval subjects and who had even written several books about army and navy life. Nevertheless, his representation of the First Minnesota Regiment in one of the most important battles of the Civil War lacks the immediacy, the sense of having been there, that distinguishes the battle scene by Pyle. It is essentially a static representation rather than a dynamic and exciting one.

So, in fact, is *Fourth Minnesota Regiment Entering Vicksburg* (fig. 97) by Francis D. Millet (1846–1912). Millet had been in charge of the mural paintings for the World's Columbian Exposition of 1893 in Chicago (where Daniel Chester French had also been well represented). The mild degree of illustrative talent he showed there was enough to earn him an invitation to paint two of the pictures for the St. Paul Capitol. The first, the Civil War scene, is a rather passive and unpretentious one. In it, however, Millet showed some artistic refinement in painting his foreground figures on a large scale in order to harmonize them with the elaborate architecture of the room and its heavy, gilded carving. The other Millet painting, which depicts the signing of the Treaty of Traverse des Sioux (fig. 98), was based on the uncompleted painting by Frank Blackwell Mayer and has been discussed previously in chapter II.

VIII Painting and Sculpture at the Turn of the Century

The building of the Minnesota State Capitol in St. Paul was a triumph of the cosmopolitan yet essentially conservative tendency of American art during the last quarter of the nineteenth century. It was a period in which a conspicuous effort was made to link American art with that of Europe and to make American artists part of the international art scene. Eclecticism, or the borrowing of styles from other times and other places, dominated American architecture. Provincial adaptations of the styles of Düsseldorf, Munich, Barbizon, and Paris were evident in American painting. Rome, Florence, and Paris were reflected in American sculpture. It was, on the whole, a gentle art geared to the domestic tastes of the wealthy businessmen who set the cultural tone of the time and was, therefore, a rather opulent art as well. Meanwhile, however, an internal pressure for change was building among the younger artists who were appearing on the scene. With the external pressure of the New York Armory Show of February, 1913, which exhibited European Fauvism, Cubism, and Expressionism, the new forms and new ideas already latent in American art received increasing attention and, ultimately, public acceptance. The show also helped to lay the groundwork for the first indigenous art movement of the New World to influence the Old, the abstract expressionism of the 1940's and 1950's.

All this is getting ahead of our story, however, and of the trends that, in the last decades of the nineteenth century and the first one of the twentieth, spread in ever-widening circles of influence from the cultural center of New York. The influence was not always one-way, though, for ideas that were germinating far from the eastern seaboard were, in turn, to influence the art produced in the great metropolitan centers of the East. Thus, the currents and crosscurrents of the nation's artistic directions were reflected in Minnesota, too, though perhaps occasionally on a paler canvas. For by the end of the century, Minnesota was no longer a frontier community but a well-established state, in every way an integral part of the national scene. Its painting and sculpture, therefore, not only mirror the wider aspect of American art but reveal its regional characteristics and contributions as well.

The year 1886 is significant in the history of art in Minnesota because in April of that year, under the sponsorship of the recently established Minneapolis Society of Fine Arts (organized in 1883), the Minneapolis School of Art was opened with Stephen A. Douglas Volk (1856–1935) as its first director. The school, the first professional one in the state, was and is a significant part of the state's artistic life.

Douglas Volk, as the son of a Massachusetts sculp-

Fig. 99. Douglas Volk. *After the Reception*, 1887. Minneapolis. Courtesy of The Minneapolis Institute of Arts. Gift of Mr. and Mrs. E. J. Phelps. Oil on canvas, 34¾ x 25½ inches.

tor, Leonard Volk, had an advantage denied most aspiring American artists of his time: early contact with a cosmopolitan circle of painters and sculptors. At the age of fourteen he was taken to Italy, where he spent a few years studying painting and drawing in Rome and Venice. Four years later he went to Paris where he entered the studio of the well-known French academic painter J. L. Gerome. By 1879 he had already exhibited at the Paris Salon of 1878 and at the Philadelphia Centennial of 1876 and had even taught at the Cooper Union School in New York. Obviously a completely professional artist and educator, he was enthusiastically received on his arrival in Minneapolis.

Volk lived in Minneapolis for seven years. Those years were spent not only in directing the affairs of Minnesota's fledgling art academy, but also in painting portraits of Minneapolis's leisure class. His *Interior with Portrait of John Scott Bradstreet* (plate 31) is a perfect vehicle for the portrayal of a cultivated gentleman of means surrounded by the proof of his discriminating taste. Bradstreet was not actually the scion of a wealthy and influential family, as his portrait would lead one to believe, but was, in the slightly disparaging phrase of the time, "in trade." He was a Minneapolis furniture and art dealer whose customers included the *nouveau riche* of the Twin Cities and surrounding area. He himself was a pioneer patron of the arts in Minnesota, a man who was genuinely interested in raising the level of culture in the rough pioneer community in which he had arrived some years earlier. His portrait stresses his position as an arbiter of taste and style, for he is as much "displayed" as are the rich carpets, exquisite furniture, and exotic bric-a-brac around him. It is just the sort of elegant portrait in sumptuous surroundings that was demanded by the wealthy middle class of the period, and the type of work that was cultivated by other artists too, John Singer Sargent, for instance, or William Merritt Chase.

Even more than the men, however, the women of the upper middle class were the subject in late nineteenth-century painting of a whole group of genre domestic pictures that portrayed both their comfortable material surroundings and their lives of fashionable leisure. Volk's *After the Reception* (fig. 99) reflects their "passive existence . . . among beautiful surroundings of French furniture, patterned wallpaper . . . silks and flowers."[1] The painting has, moreover, a strong narrative base, for it describes vividly, if indirectly, the rigors of the fashionable wedding reception just ended. The weary bride,[2] still in her wedding dress and satin slippers, rests on a delicate settee amidst the elegant confusion of filmy tulle and wilted blossoms. It is all extremely graceful, charming, and domestic, projecting just the image of well-bred inactivity that contemporary American culture held as the feminine ideal.

The enthusiasm with which Volk was welcomed to Minneapolis did not apparently produce the number of painting commissions he had hoped for, and in 1893 he returned to New York to teach at the Art Students League. His connection with Minnesota was not completely severed, however; for, as we have seen, when the new State Capitol was decorated in 1905, he was awarded two painting commissions for the governor's reception room. *The Battle of Mission Ridge* and *Father Hennepin Discovering the Falls of St. Anthony* when contrasted with *After the Reception* throw into sharp relief the nineteenth century's polarity between masculine activity, on the one hand, and feminine passivity on the other.

In 1893 when Volk left, he recommended to the Board of Trustees that Robert Koehler (1850–1917) be appointed the new director of the Minneapolis School of Art. Koehler was, in many ways, a much more original painter than Volk. He was a man of liberal attitudes and, for that time, even radical ideas about both society and art. Nevertheless, after serving for one year as an instructor in the Minneapolis School of Art, he was appointed its director in 1894.

Koehler, like Volk, had had a solid international education in the arts by the time he arrived in Minneapolis in 1893. He was born in Hamburg, Germany, but spent his childhood in Milwaukee, where his family moved in 1854. When he was fifteen, he was apprenticed to a firm of lithographers there, but in 1871 he moved to Pittsburgh and then to New York, where he attended classes at the National Academy of Design and at the Art Students League. From 1873 to 1875 he was a student at the Munich Academy of Fine Arts under Ludwig von Löfftz, but in 1875 lack of funds forced him to return to New York, where he resumed study at the Art Students League. In 1879, under the patronage of a wealthy New York brewer, he returned to Munich and remained there for the next thirteen years. He became president of the Munich Artists Association on whose behalf he organized the American section of the international art exhibitions held in 1883 and 1888. In 1888 he even organized an art school in Munich, but in 1892 he was back in New York, where he was living at the time of his invitation to come to Minneapolis.

Koehler brought with him to Minneapolis an important picture he had painted in Germany some years before. Called *The Strike* (plate 32), it was based on the memory of a railroad workers' strike Koehler had seen in Pittsburgh in 1877. After some coaxing, but still rather surprisingly, the Minneapolis Society of Fine Arts, whose well-heeled members do not seem to have read the painting's implications clearly, bought the work in 1901. It was presented by them to the city of Minneapolis and hung for many years in the public library. *The Strike* is one of the first major American paintings to depict the early history of the labor movement and the struggle of the working classes against capitalist society.[3] Other painters had already begun to draw attention to urban life and industrialized society; John Ferguson Wier, Thomas Anshutz, and Charles Frederick Ulrich were notable among them. Their pictures were precursors of the so-called Ashcan School of the early twentieth century and especially of Robert Henri and George Luks, who focused their attention on the urban poor. Koehler's painting was unusual for its time, however, in pointing specifically to the conflict inherent in nineteenth-century industrialization. Indeed, his possible connection with contemporary European "realists" like Hubert von Herkomer in England and Adolf von Menzel in Germany should be investigated, for it might reveal more widespread social protest in the

arts than previously suspected.[4] If Douglas Volk depicted the pleasant, even luxurious results of the growth of industry and commerce in the late nineteenth century, Koehler and some of his European colleagues were looking at the darker aspects of contemporary economics. What they saw and how they felt about it were graphically described in a number of significant pictures, like *The Strike*, which were the first to call attention to the human misery spawned by the factory system and the urban environment.

During his Minneapolis years, however, Koehler seems to have devoted himself to subjects of less momentous social significance. Instead, he painted pleasant landscapes of Minneapolis and the surrounding area and numerous portraits of family, friends, and civic and intellectual leaders. He was (on more than one occasion) his own subject as well, as his sensitive *Self-Portrait* reveals (fig. 100). His *Rainy Evening on Hennepin Avenue* (plate 33), painted about 1910, combines portraiture of a sort (the woman and child in the foreground are his wife, Marie, and his son, Edwin, with the family dog) with a view of Minneapolis's main street as it looked about 1910. The painting's subtle color harmonies and soft, moisture-laden atmosphere recall the works of the expatriate American master of tone and cadence James Abbott McNeill Whistler. In Koehler's picture, however, form does not dissolve, as it does so often in Whistler's work, but retains its solid, three-dimensional quality in the damp haze of the city's dusk.

Something of the loose and sketchy brushwork characteristic of the Munich Academy, in revolt against the tight realism of Düsseldorf, is revealed in a number of Koehler's small landscape and portrait studies. His *Head of an Old Woman* (fig. 101), painted in Munich, captures with a few sure strokes and in a thick impasto the image of old age. He later used the same loose and sketchy style in his landscape *At Lake Minnetonka* (fig. 102), which depicts a cloudy late summer day on the shore of Minneapolis's largest suburban lake. In both of these paintings, Koehler shows a characteristic directness in his approach to his subject, a lack of affectation that derived, in part at least,

Fig. 100. Robert Koehler. *Self-Portrait*, 1898.
New York. Private collection.
Oil on canvas, 38½ x 23 inches.

Fig. 101. Robert Koehler. *Head of an Old Woman*, 1881.
Minneapolis. Courtesy of The Minneapolis Institute of Arts.
Gift of the Art School Students.
Oil on canvas, 18 x 14½ inches.

from Munich aesthetics. The representation of the real rather than the ideal was also the goal of New York's Ashcan School, a group of painters sometimes called "The Eight," who were staging their own revolt against the American academic tradition. They represented the most progressive trend in American painting in the first part of the twentieth century, and Koehler, by sharing their social concern and their espousal of "real life" aesthetics, placed himself squarely in their camp. Furthermore, in his position as director of Minnesota's own "academy," he spread their new gospel of American art, even while it was still being formulated, to Minnesota and its art community.

An interesting combination of several contemporary trends is to be found in Alexander Grinager's *Boys Bathing* (plate 34). Grinager (1865–1949) was born in Albert Lea, Minnesota, to a family of Norwegian immigrants. His early efforts at painting were portraits of local Indians, though none of these seem to have survived. Determined to pursue a career in art, the young Grinager entered the studio of Peter Clau-

Fig. 102. Robert Koehler. *At Lake Minnetonka*, before 1901. Milwaukee.
Private collection. Oil on canvas, 17¾ x 24 inches.

sen, where he received his first formal instruction in painting. He apparently came to share Clausen's penchant for stage design—a liking that was characteristic, as we have seen, of many early Minnesota painters and that was reflected in the "panorama fever" of the 1860's to 1880's—for in later life Grinager accepted many commissions for mural painting, hotel decoration, and stage and scene design. In any event, after his initial study with Clausen, Grinager left in 1887 for Europe, where he studied first in Copenhagen and then in Paris in the Académie Julien under Jean Paul Laurens and Benjamin Constant. Later he traveled to Italy and Sicily. Though he lived in Minneapolis again in the early 1890's, after 1896 he made his permanent home in Ossining, New York.

Boys Bathing, painted in 1894 before Grinager left Minnesota for the East, reveals the influence of the "plein air" movement and the brushwork and broken color of the French Impressionists. Grinager was especially fascinated by the technique of Monet and his ability to capture the transient quality of light in nature. He was not, of course, the only painter of his time to bring the techniques of Impressionism back to America. Others, better known, had already done so; the names of Childe Hassam and John Henry Twachtman come readily to mind. Grinager was influential, nevertheless, in bringing the sunny palettes and light-filled canvases of the French Impressionists to the attention of Minnesota audiences, painters and patrons alike, and thus he, like Koehler, helped to make the area aware of the new developments shaping the national art scene.

Grinager's picture depicts a group of boys in various stages of undress about to enjoy the cool waters of the Mississippi River on a sunlit summer day. The boys were the sons of poor Irish and Scandinavian immigrants, a number of whom lived at that time in a shanty town at the east end of the old Washington Avenue Bridge. The scene is of the river flats below the bridge, near an old stone quarry that existed then and served as a welcome playground for the neighborhood boys. The picture has the high, or rather nonexistent, horizon line typical of many French Impres-

sionist paintings and has their broken color technique as well. But though the study of light in nature is typical of the French Impressionists, the depiction of five ragamuffins of poor immigrant families is not. The Impressionists were, by and large, painters of the leisure activities of the Parisian middle class and of each other and, with a few rare exceptions, shunned any suggestion of social comment. Grinager's painting is interesting, therefore, as a Minnesota counterpart to the work of such American "realists" as Thomas Eakins and George Bellows, both of whom revealed in similar types of paintings their interest in the unidealized human figure as much as in the study of light in nature.[5]

One other contemporary painter, and a far more prolific one, was even more closely identified with Minnesota than Grinager. He was Alexis Jean Fournier (1865–1948), who, though born in St. Paul, had spent his early youth in Milwaukee. He returned to Minneapolis in 1883, supporting himself as a sign and scenery painter until, under the sponsorship of a number of Minneapolis patrons of the arts, he was able to enroll as a student in the Minneapolis School of Art. He may well have been one of Douglas Volk's first students there. In 1887 Fournier established his own studio in Minneapolis and devoted himself to producing a large body of oils, water colors, and drawings. In 1893, again with the aid of his wealthy Minneapolis patrons, Fournier at last left for Paris, where, like so many of his compatriots he enrolled at the conservative Académie Julien under Jean Paul Laurens, Benjamin Constant, and Henri Harpignies. The latter, especially, was to have a lasting influence on the young Minnesota artist. Harpignies was a follower of the French Barbizon School, a painter of idyllic landscapes composed with great elegance and style. After returning to Minneapolis and living there for a number of years, Fournier went back to France, took up residence in the village of Barbizon near the ancient forest of Fontainebleau, and in 1908 undertook a major project of twenty canvases in the Barbizon mood. Called *Haunts and Home of the Barbizon Masters*, the project emphasized his identification with the school of landscape painters who had led French artists in the 1830's to an appreciation of the beauties of nature in all its atmospheric moods, thus laying the groundwork for French Impressionism. Most of Fournier's Minnesota paintings belong, however, to his earlier period, when he painted the local scene in a more direct and even matter-of-fact style.

For local history buffs, Fournier's pictures of early Minneapolis and St. Paul are particularly interesting in that they offer still recognizable views of city landmarks. They are instructive stylistically, too, when compared with other and earlier views of the same subject. Fournier's large and ambitious picture of Fort Snelling (plate 35), painted in 1888, is a case in point. The fort had often, as we have seen, caught the attention of local and traveling artists, for situated as it is high above the confluence of two scenic rivers, it possessed both historic and pictorial importance. Thus, earlier artists had tended to romanticize the subject and to offer "picturesque" views of the fort on its commanding promontory. This is even true of a contemporary though more traditional artist than Fournier, William Henry Hyde (1858–1943). Hyde was a New York landscape painter of essentially conservative tendencies, who traveled through Minnesota in the late nineteenth century painting its scenic spots. His picture of Fort Snelling (fig. 103) was painted about 1890, but he takes the same distant and idealized view of it as earlier artists had. Hyde still emphasizes the wilderness aspect of the fort, as though it were still a military outpost on a remote frontier. Beneath a vast and glowing sky the fort is reflected in the quiet waters of the river, and the land itself stretches in infinite space to the distant horizon. This is, in fact, a late example of the poetic "luminist" landscapes of the earlier romantic tradition. Fournier's representation is far different. For one thing, the artist's vantage point is below the fort instead of at a distance overlooking it. This is important because it puts the observer in a more direct and immediate relationship with the subject, pulling him inside the picture, as it were, instead of maintaining his distance outside of it. The low vantage point has the effect,

moreover, of filling up much of the canvas, thus avoiding the vast and lustrous skies of the romantics. The light itself is more natural. It suggests the clear and unambiguous light of an ordinary day, rather than the stagey glow of an idealized and dramatic moment. The untidy shore (with the scattered remains of an early wooden bridge—replaced now by an iron one high above the river), the shallow riverbed, and the grazing sheep at the foot of the hill all emphasize the genre quality of Fournier's painting and its focus on the ordinary. In this lies its significant contrast with the out-of-the-ordinary perception of the scene by other artists of more romantic temperaments.

Fournier's *Lowry Hill* (fig. 104) also evokes a response of instant recognition. The view is toward the northwest from the point on Lowry Hill where a freeway interchange now carries heavy traffic from Minneapolis to the south and east. None of the buildings seen in the picture are still standing, though the contours of the land remain unchanged and the flat horizon still stretches away to the northern edges of the city. The strong light and shadow reflected from a partly clouded sky create a feeling of transience, a moment in the city's history between provincial backwater and modern metropolis. Here, too, Fournier succeeds in creating an impression of immediate, almost tangible relationship between the observer and the pictured scene.

Even when it came to painting a more historic landmark such as the original Chapel of St. Paul (fig. 105), built in 1841 by the pioneer missionary Father Lucian Galtier, Fournier limited his editorial comments to a few Indian tepees in the background and an emphasis on the crudeness of the log cabin church. An even greater clarity and directness is evident in his painting of the first courthouse in St. Paul (fig. 106), which was built in the approved neoclassic manner with imposing columns and pediment. The building illustrates, in fact, the transition from a small pioneer settlement to a settled and growing city, able to afford the latest revival style in its public buildings.

Fournier's interest in the local scene was seemingly limitless. A fine picture of the Mill Pond at Minneapo-

Fig. 103. William Henry Hyde. *Ft. Snelling*, c. 1890. St. Paul. Courtesy of
Minnesota Historical Society. Oil on canvas, 18 x 30 inches.

lis (plate 36), dated 1888, was painted from what today would be the western end of the Third Avenue
Bridge looking approximately east.[6] It shows the recently completed stone arch bridge of the St. Paul,
Minneapolis and Manitoba Railroad Co. (later Bur-
lington–Great Northern). Beyond it is an old steel
truss that used to carry Tenth Avenue traffic across
the river. The building just showing on the left is the
"Exposition Building," illustrated in many old pictures
of Minneapolis. It combined Gothic, Islamic, and other styles in one fascinatingly eclectic mélange. On the
right are the polygonal buildings that were the origi-

nal gas tanks of the Minneapolis Gas Company and
to their left, just breaking the horizon line, are the
first buildings of the University of Minnesota campus. From the campus Fournier painted the scene
shown in figure 107 of the view looking northwest toward downtown Minneapolis. The most striking of his
many local pictures, however, is the one painted in
1889, *Lake Harriet by Moonlight* (plate 37). Here the
artist contrasted the cold light of the moon and its
silvery reflection in the lake with the warm glow of the
lamplight illuminating the people sitting in the lakeside pavilion. It is a dramatic and unusual picture and

Fig. 104. Alexis Jean Fournier. *Lowry Hill, Minneapolis*, July, 1888. Minneapolis. Courtesy of The Minneapolis Institute of Arts. The Julia B. Bigelow Fund. Oil on canvas, 16¼ x 24 inches.

Fig. 105.
Alexis Jean Fournier. *Chapel of St. Paul.*
St. Paul. Courtesy of Minnesota
Historical Society.
Oil on canvas, 28 x 46 inches.

Fig. 106.
Alexis Jean Fournier. *Ramsey
County Courthouse.* St. Paul. Courtesy of
Minnesota Historical Society.
Oil on canvas, 30 x 36 inches.

Fig. 107. Alexis Jean Fournier. *Minneapolis from University Campus*, July, 1888. Minneapolis.
Courtesy of University of Minnesota Gallery. Oil on canvas, 16⅛ x 28 inches.

Fig. 108. Edwin M. Dawes. *Channel to the Mills*, 1913. Minneapolis. Courtesy of The Minneapolis Institute of Arts. Anonymous gift. Oil on canvas, 51 x 39½ inches.

one that emphasizes Fournier's position as an important nineteenth-century American painter.

Edwin M. Dawes (1872–1934), like Fournier, painted the early Minneapolis scene, though in a softer, more atmospheric style. His *Channel to the Mills* (fig. 108) of 1913 is an impressionistic representation of the cold Minnesota climate, but it is not, of course, a study of nature. In the background rise the hazy yet monumental forms of Minneapolis's flour mills, one of the major sources of its wealth and importance. Unlike Fournier's, Dawes's cityscape dissolves in a shimmer of smoke and mist. It thus romanticizes the promise of prosperity and progress associated by some with increasing industrialization. The picture shows the bright side of American industry in contrast with Koehler's pessimistic view of conflict within it. Dawes, an Iowa-born artist, worked in Minnesota during his early career but left the area in his middle age to settle in California.

Other turn-of-the-century artists were associated with Minnesota for even briefer periods. Homer Dodge Martin (1836–1897), a New York landscapist in the French Barbizon tradition, lived in and near St. Paul from 1893 to his death in 1897. Some of his greatest canvases were produced in a quiet Minnesota farmhouse during this period. They include his well-known *Harp of the Winds*, which is not a Minnesota scene at all but an idyll of the French countryside. Some sixteen years later, in 1913, another eastern artist, Rockwell Kent (1882–1971), lived briefly in Winona, leaving after a year to make his reputation in other parts of the world. There were others who came and went. Katherine Merrill (b. 1876) of Milwaukee and Chicago painted the granddaughters of General Le-Duc (fig. 109), a well-known Hastings pioneer, in a style reminiscent of Mary Cassatt. All these artists helped to maintain Minnesota's ties with the eastern centers of culture and style. By the outbreak of the First World War the eddies of influence containing new ideas of form and subject matter—ideas stimulated and publicized by the Armory Show of 1913—began to be felt in Minnesota, too, bringing it solidly into the new century. The career of sculptor Paul Man-

Fig. 109. Katherine Merrill. *Granddaughters of General LeDuc*, 1890's. Hastings. Collection of Carroll B. Simmons. Oil on canvas, 26½ x 21½ inches.

ship (1885–1966) illustrates this transition, for if the eclectic realism of his early work ties him to the romanticism of the nineteenth century, his mature pieces reveal an interest in the purely formal problems of mass and line that characterize so much of twentieth-century aesthetics.

Paul Manship received his earliest training in art in his native St. Paul, first at the Mechanic Arts High School and later at the St. Paul Institute of Arts. In 1905 he left home to study at the Art Students League in New York, where he also worked as an assistant to the sculptor Solon Borglum. The next year found him studying under Charles Grafly at the Pennsylvania Academy of Fine Arts. In 1909 while acting as assistant to the sculptor Isidore Konti, he won the coveted American Prix de Rome, a scholarship to the American Academy there. It was in Rome that Manship formed his early style and developed his love for mythological subjects. It was there, too, that he perfected his craftsmanship and found inspiration in the art of ancient—even archaic—Greece and Rome, as well as in the Renaissance sculpture of Italy. But Manship brought his own creative impulses to bear on these disparate artistic sources and out of them created a style that was both personal and contemporary.

Among Manship's early works—and only these fall within the scope of this book—is a statuette executed in Rome in 1912 called *Playfulness* (fig. 110). Here the artist reveals both the strong tendency toward the archaic of his early style and a taste for the purely decorative which gradually subordinates itself to form in his later work. There is a free and lighthearted exuberance here, which, like that in much of Manship's sculpture, is combined with a rhythmic sense of movement and an energetic flow of line from the mother's upturned toe, through the pixie face of her child, to the tight coil of hair waving behind her. The same graceful line and inspiration from the antique characterize Manship's *Lyric Muse* (fig. 111) of the same year. It is quieter in mood, as befits the subject, and a more self-contained piece, but here, too, one feels a suppressed energy that is expressed in song instead of in physical movement.

An interesting piece made two years later is Man-

ship's sculpture-portrait of his infant daughter, *Pauline Frances* (fig. 112), done in 1914. The obvious source of his inspiration here was the child portraits of such Italian Renaissance sculptors as Mino da Fiesole, Donatello, and Desiderio da Settignano. None of these, however, would have executed such a starkly realistic portrait. Theirs would have been more idealized, more remote, and, in a sense, less personal. Though trappings of the Renaissance are there—in the frame, the pedestal, the garlands, and cherub decoration—the sculpture is, like all of Manship's work, an intensely individual adaptation of previous forms to suit his own artistic purpose.

Nor would anyone mistake *Gnome* (fig. 113) of 1914 for anything other than a twentieth-century sculpture. Conceived as part of a fountain commissioned by the American Academy in Rome, it combines the decorative, linear patterns typical of the primitive, or archaic, artist with the feeling for abstract form in space which characterizes the art of this century. Indeed, the figure expresses with style, grace, and no little wit the bridge between the art of the past and the aesthetics of the future, as is often the case in the work of Minnesota's best known early twentieth-century sculptor.

Manship's work, then, illustrates many of the typical features of Minnesota's art before the Armory Show of 1913. It was eclectic, borrowing inspiration from many different periods and styles. It reflected aesthetic ideas that were to be found in other parts of the country. It revealed a concern for quality craftsmanship that is one of the legacies of the many excellent artists and artisans who worked in the state. Manship's training in the East and in Europe is also typical, with its lessons from the past and its new ideas pointing to the aesthetics of the future. After the Armory Show and First World War, Minnesota's painting and sculpture, like American art generally, became more and more a part of the international art scene while yet retaining some characteristically regional features. Its story—from 1914 to the present—forms a separate chapter in the history of American art, and one that has yet to be written.

Fig. 110. Paul Manship. *Playfulness*, 1912. Washington, D.C.
Courtesy of National Collection of Fine Arts,
Smithsonian Institution. Bronze with marble base,
12½ x 12½ inches.

Fig. 111. Paul Manship. *Lyric Muse*, 1912. St. Paul.
Courtesy of Minnesota Museum of Art. Bronze, height 11¾ inches,
base length 7 inches, width 5½ inches.

Fig. 112. Paul Manship. *Pauline Frances*, 1914.
St. Paul. Courtesy of Minnesota Museum of Art.
Plaster, polychromed, height 20¾ inches.

Fig. 113. Paul Manship. *Gnome*, 1914 (cast in
bronze, 1955). Washington, D.C. Courtesy
of National Collection of·Fine Arts, Smithsonian
Institution. Bronze with marble base, height 7 inches.

Notes, Appendix, and Selected Bibliography

Notes

Introduction

1. William H. Keating, professor of mineralogy and geology at the University of Pennsylvania, also accompanied the expedition. His account of it was published in Philadelphia in 1824 under the title *Narrative of an Expedition to the Source of St. Peter's River, Lake Winnipeek, Lake of the Woods, etc. Performed in the Year 1823.*

I Explorers

1. Titian Ramsey Peale (1799–1885), a son of the Philadelphia artist Charles Willson Peale (1741–1827), was probably the first professional painter of the trans-Mississippi West. He was a member of Major Stephen H. Long's earlier expedition in 1819 to the Rocky Mountains. Samuel Seymour served as official artist to both that expedition and the later one of 1823 to the upper Mississippi.
2. An engraving after Seymour's sketch is reproduced in Bertha L. Heilbron's "Frontier Artists," *American Heritage*, Winter, 1950, p. A9H.
3. This is reproduced in *Kennedy Quarterly*, June, 1973, p. 173.
4. For a fuller discussion of the development of this iconographic theme, see Rena N. Coen, "The Last of the Buffalo," *American Art Journal*, November, 1973, pp. 83–94.
5. George Catlin, *North American Indians, Being Letters and Notes on Their Manners & Customs, Written during Eight Years Travel amongst the Wildest Tribes of Indians in North America*, 2 vols. (London, 1841), I:3.
6. *Ibid.*, p. 261.
7. *Ibid.*, p. 260.

8. The O'Fallon portrait, acquired some years ago by San Francisco's Maxwell Galleries, is not signed either. It was sold to the Maxwell Galleries by a direct descendant of Major O'Fallon. The O'Fallon family maintained that the picture was done by Catlin, an attribution strengthened by the fact that O'Fallon and Catlin were known to have been friends. Furthermore, O'Fallon commissioned Catlin to paint the portraits of Indian chiefs of the Missouri Territory. O'Fallon was also a nephew of General William Clark, whose portrait is signed and dated (1832) by Catlin.
9. See Catlin, *North American Indians*, 2:135ff., and Lawrence Taliaferro, *Journals*, June 24, 1829; July 27, 1835; August 17, 21, and September 5, 1836 (available on microfilm at the Minnesota Historical Society, St. Paul).
10. Catlin, *North American Indians*, 1:2.
11. As Taliaferro was reluctant to record personal matters in the *Journals* other than those related directly to the business of the agency, Mrs. Taliaferro is rarely mentioned. There is, therefore, no information in them about the portrait. Nevertheless, a link to Bingham should be considered in the following backward sequence of events. In 1946 both Taliaferro portraits were given to the Minnesota Historical Society by Mrs. Frank Pesch (née Bonner) of Clayton, Missouri. Mrs. Pesch's mother was a niece and ward of the Taliaferros. In 1857 she married Samuel Bonner in Virginia and moved with him to St. Louis. Taliaferro was also, incidentally, a Virginian. In 1841 Bingham

signed and dated a portrait of the child Jesse Heath in Petersburg, Virginia. His mother's maiden name was Margaret Bonner. (This information is from the registrar's files, Minnesota Historical Society, St. Paul.)

12. See Robert Taft, *Artists and Illustrators of the Old West 1850–1900* (New York, 1953), p. 15. An engraving after Stanley's *View of St. Paul* is reproduced in Bertha L. Heilbron's "Frontier Artists," *American Heritage*, Winter, 1950, p. A12H.

13. Taft, *Artists and Illustrators*, p. 273, n. 44. Strobel's *View of St. Paul* is reproduced in I. N. Phelps Stokes and Daniel C. Haskell, *American Historical Prints* (New York, 1933), Plate 85a.

14. The painting, a large one, measuring 3½ x 4 feet, hangs in the attic of the Sibley House in Mendota, now owned by the Minnesota Chapter of the Daughters of the American Revolution. It is a profile view of the dog who fills up almost the entire space of the canvas, and it is signed "Char. Deas pinxit." The picture is in poor condition with a bullet hole where Lion's eye should be. It is a good example of an important painting left to molder away because of the neglect of its owners who, in this case, even refused permission to photograph the painting.

15. It is interesting that after Deas became mentally ill in 1849 he painted a number of pictures, now lost, based on themes similar to Fuseli's. Thus Fuseli's *The Madhouse* (British Museum), engraved by Thomas Holloway for the English edition of J. K. Lavater's *Essays on Physiognomy* (London, 1792), might have inspired a Deas painting captioned *The Maniac*, exhibited in 1859 in the Chicago Exhibition of Fine Arts. Similarly, a Deas painting entitled *The Vision*, exhibited in 1849 at the National Academy of Design, was undoubtedly inspired by Fuseli's *The Nightmare* (Detroit Institute of Arts), which was published in a color aquatint by Thomas Burke in 1802. Tuckerman described *The Vision* as "representing a black sea, over which a figure hung, suspended by a ring, while from the waves a monster was springing, was [*sic*] so horrible, that a sensitive artist fainted at the sight." See Henry T. Tuckerman, *Book of the Artists: American Artist Life* (New York, 1867), p. 429.

II Soldiers

1. Colonel Henry Leavenworth actually commanded the expedition that set up camp at the site preparatory to the building of the fort. He was shortly succeeded by Colonel Snelling.

2. The best known of these is *Dahcotah; or, Life and Legends of the Sioux around Fort Snelling* (New York,

1849). A number of Mrs. Eastman's stories were also published in *The Talisman* and other gift books. These were volumes of stories, articles, and illustrations considered appropriate for feminine consumption in the nineteenth century.

3. The detail of an Indian encampment in the background of Eastman's painting bears a significant similarity to a similar detail in *The Last of the Mohicans* (Wadsworth Atheneum) by Thomas Cole, the founder of the Hudson River School. Both pictures represent episodes in Indian life, whether real or fictional, as minute and distant elements in the vast magnificence of the American wilderness.

4. See Rena N. Coen, "Edward K. Thomas: Fort Snelling Artist," *Minnesota History*, Fall, 1969, pp. 317–326.

5. Several versions of Thomas's view of Fort Snelling exist, including one at the Minnesota Historical Society and one at the Sibley House in Mendota.

6. Charles A. Dana, *The United States Illustrated*, as quoted in Perry T. Rathbone, ed., *Westward the Way* (St. Louis, 1954), p. 222.

7. David L. Kingsbury, "Sully's Expedition against the Sioux, 1864," *Minnesota Historical Society Collections* 8(1898):449–462.

8. The manuscript and Sully's sketches are in the Coe Collection (IV, 442) in the Collection of Western Americana Books and Manuscripts, Beinecke Library, Yale University.

9. Quoted in Bertha L. Heilbron, *With Pen and Pencil on the Frontier in 1851* (St. Paul, 1932), p. 3.

10. *Ibid.*, p. 4.

11. See Marvin Ross, *The West of Alfred Jacob Miller* (Norman, Okla., 1968).

12. The drawing is a portrait of Nancy McLure, who was the daughter of an Indian mother and Lieutenant James McLure of Fort Snelling.

13. Heilbron, *With Pen and Pencil*, p. 20.

III Painters of the Panorama

1. Lee Marius Schoonmaker, *John Vanderlyn, Artist, 1775–1852* (Kingston, N.Y., 1950). William Winstanley, an English painter, displayed the first panorama in America in 1775.

2. Bertha L. Heilbron, *Making a Motion Picture in 1848* (St. Paul, 1936). Miss Heilbron notes (p. 16) that the Banvard panorama pictured the Mississippi only from the mouth of the Missouri to the Gulf and that some further sections were added later. A further section of the upper Mississippi which was shown to American audiences during Banvard's absence abroad in 1850 was not his work.

3. Eight of the sketches were probably acquired by Lewis on a visit to Fort Snelling in 1848. Nine more may have been given to him later in the same year when Mrs. Eastman was in Cincinnati to arrange with Lewis, who was there at the time, for Eastman's paintings to be exhibited at the Cincinnati Art Union. Cf. John Francis McDermott, *Seth Eastman's Mississippi, a Lost Panorama Recovered* (Urbana, Ill., 1973).

4. Lewis's panorama was a critical success but a commercial failure. Lewis continued to exhibit it in Europe until 1854 and then determined to sell it. Its subsequent history is appropriately exotic. It was bought in 1857 by a wealthy Dutch planter, named Hermans, from the island of Java. After a long delay and with only half of what he owed Lewis paid, Hermans sailed for Calcutta in 1860 with the panorama safely in his baggage. According to an account published in 1881, and perhaps fictitious, the panorama was displayed in India and then taken to Java, where one of the native princes bought it. The story explains that "when he wishes to offer a guest an unusual treat, he has the Mississippi River unwound from its roller while he explains its beauties." The panorama subsequently disappeared into the hidden mysteries of the Far East. See the introduction by Bertha L. Heilbron, ed., to Henry Lewis, *The Valley of the Mississippi Illustrated*, trans. A. Hermina Poatgieter (St. Paul, 1967), pp. 7–8.

5. It is possible that Lewis actually went to Düsseldorf, at least in part, to carry out a tentative agreement made five years earlier in St. Louis with the German publisher of his book, Heinrich Arnz, of Arnz and Company, who had been in America in 1848. It is possible that Arnz was looking for an artist-author who could produce an illustrated book about the Mississippi River. See Heilbron's introduction to *The Valley of the Mississippi*, pp. 8–9.

6. Heilbron, *Making a Motion Picture*, pp. 8–9.

7. *Ibid.*, p. 9.

IV Tourists and Travelers

1. Theodore C. Blegen, *Grass Roots History* (Minneapolis, 1947), pp. 122–123.

2. Schoolcraft's contribution to the popularization of the oral literature of the Indians is generally acknowledged; Mary Eastman's is not as well known. For a discussion of Longfellow's indebtedness to Schoolcraft, see Chase S. and Stellanova Osborn, *Schoolcraft, Longfellow, Hiawatha* (Lancaster, Pa., 1942), and Mentor Williams, ed., *Schoolcraft's Indian Legends* (East Lansing, Mich., 1956).

3. This is according to William Walton, who wrote a biography of Johnson shortly after the latter's death. See Patricia Hills, *Eastman Johnson* (New York, 1972), p. 17.

4. When the paintings were given to the city of Duluth by Mr. Richard T. Crane (who bought them in 1908 from the artist's widow), a collection of Indian garments purchased by Eastman Johnson at Grand Portage in 1857 was included with the pictures. One of them is the dark blue robe worn by the sitter for *Hiawatha*. It was held in place by red shoulder straps worked in a design of white beads and trimmed with green, red, and white tape. It is usually displayed underneath the picture of Hiawatha by the St. Louis County Historical Society, where the Eastman Johnson collection now resides.

5. See Hills, *Eastman Johnson*, p. 24.

6. This is probably the same George F. Fuller whose painting *A Steamboat Race on the Mississippi River (between the Baltic and Diana)* was lithographed by A. Weingartner in New York in 1859. (See Harry T. Peters, *America on Stone* [Garden City, N.Y., 1931], p. 192, pl. 105.) The Minnesota scenes also include the middle initial "F." in the signature. As the well-known George Fuller retired into full-time farming before reemerging as a serious artist in 1875, it is possible that in those long, intervening years he simply dropped the middle initial from his signed works. A further connection linking George Fuller to Minnesota is the arrival of his cousin Jonas Holland Howe in Minnesota in 1854 (the year after Fuller's visit to the territory) to take up farming and practice art as an avocation. (See chapter V.)

7. John Francis McDermott, "Minnesota 100 Years Ago," *Minnesota History*, Autumn, 1952, p. 112.

8. *Ibid.*, p. 123.

9. Barbara Novak, *American Painting of the Nineteenth Century* (New York, 1969).

10. In 1840 Kensett saw an exhibition of George Catlin's Indian portraits in London and was very impressed by them. Perhaps it was then that he determined to visit the Minnesota Territory.

11. An 1869 painting by Duncanson called *Waiting for a Shot* (illustrated in *Kennedy Quarterly*, June, 1971, pl. 15) of a lonely buffalo hunter on the Great Plains seems to indicate that Duncanson traveled fairly extensively in the Middle West.

12. Alfred Lord Tennyson, "The Lotos-Eaters." It is known that Duncanson produced a "painted poem" based on these lines. See James A. Porter, *Modern Negro Art* (New York, 1943), pp. 43–46.

13. Both of these Meeker paintings are reproduced in the *Kennedy Quarterly*, April, 1971, pp. 233–234.

14. Conway's *Buffalo in a Blizzard* (*Kennedy Quarterly*, June, 1973, p. 233) is even more impressionistic.
15. See Jeffrey R. Brown, *Alfred Thompson Bricher, 1837–1908* (Indianapolis Museum of Art, Catalogue of Exhibition, September 12–October 23, 1973), p. 13.
16. *Ibid.*, p. 16.
17. As quoted by Bertha L. Heilbron, "Edwin Whitefield, Settlers' Artist," *Minnesota History*, Summer, 1966, p. 64.
18. *Ibid.*, p. 73.

V Settlers: The Primitives

1. Emma Lazarus, "The New Colossus."
2. Jonas Holland Howe is described in an article by Norman A. Geske, "Jonas Holland Howe, a Pioneer Minnesota Artist," *Minnesota History*, Fall, 1950, pp. 99–104.
3. I am indebted to Professor Marion J. Nelson for having brought this altarpiece to my attention and for generously sharing with me his current research on it.
4. Rein was a member of an orchestra called "The Scandinavian Hillbillies," which was directed by Thorsten Skarning in the early years of this century.
5. Marion J. Nelson, "A Pioneer Artist and His Masterpiece," *Norwegian-American Studies*, 1965, pp. 3–17.
6. *Ibid.*

VI Settlers: The Professionals

1. Reprinted in *Minneapolis Morning Tribune*, March 8, 1948.
2. Marion J. Nelson has written about this artist in "Herbjørn Gausta, Norwegian-American Painter," *Studies in Scandinavian-American Interrelations*, 1971, pp. 1–24.
3. Adolf Tidemand's *Haugianerne*, or "The Followers of Hauge," of 1848.
4. Quoted by Nelson, "Herbjørn Gausta," p. 10.
5. *The Lay Preacher* bears an interesting relation to Degas's *Absinthe* of 1876. There is a distant similarity of figures and table and a similar unidealized, though sympathetic, approach to the somber subject matter.
6. *Dalles Visitor*, Summer, 1973. I am indebted to Mrs. Helen M. White of Taylors Falls for having provided me with information concerning this artist.
7. The authorship of the painting poses an intriguing puzzle. It is signed Herbert L.(?) Conner. A Herbert G. Conner is mentioned in a *St. Paul Dispatch* obituary notice on July 11, 1933. This Conner arrived in St. Paul in 1880 and worked for many years as a newspaper artist and cartoonist for the *St. Paul Globe*. He also painted portraits of Minnesota dignitaries and was interested enough in the history of the state to have painted a picture called "*Pig's Eye*" *Parent Ar-*

riving at Fountain Cave in 1839, which he presented to the St. Paul Elk's Club. As a newspaper artist he may have been interested enough in the story of the *Manistee* (which he could easily have run across in the newspaper office) to have painted a picture in memory of it. The *Manistee* painting is dated 1897.
8. They were Captain John McKay and Chief Engineer Daniel Stringer, but it is not known which portrait is which. The ship belonged to the Lake Superior and South Shore Line.
9. George P. A. Healy's chatty and self-congratulatory autobiography is entitled *Reminiscences of a Portrait Painter* (Chicago, 1894). A scarcely less admiring book but including a fuller account of his life was written by his granddaughter Marie de Mare (*G. P. A. Healy, American Artist* [New York, 1954]).
10. It is, of course, possible that Healy, who was constantly traveling, may have visited St. Paul in 1861 when the Rice portraits were painted. It is more likely, however, that they were painted in Washington.

VII The Capitol

1. Neil B. Thompson, *Minnesota's State Capitol* (St. Paul, 1974), p. 56.
2. *Ibid.*, p. 56.
3. The title of the second lunette is usually listed as *The Relation of the Individual to the State*, but La Farge himself gave the title *The Relation of the Moral Law to the State* to the water-color sketch upon which the finished painting is based.

VIII Painting and Sculpture at the Turn of the Century

1. Patricia Hills, *The Painters' America: Rural and Urban Life, 1810–1910* (New York, 1974), p. 97. There is a good discussion in Hills's book of the artists who painted this aspect of late nineteenth-century American life. Among them are William McGregor Paxton, Frank Weston Benson, Edmund Tarbell, and Julian Alden Weir.
2. The bride was Caroline Keith Thompson, whose parents were Minneapolis friends of Douglas Volk's.
3. Even earlier, in 1855, Koehler had exhibited *The Socialist* at the National Academy of Design.
4. Adolf von Menzel's *The Public Funeral of the Victims of the March Revolution, 1848* is especially interesting in this connection for both its ideological and its pictorial similarities to Koehler's painting. Hubert von Herkomer also painted themes of social protest. His 1891 picture, *On Strike*, depicted an idle workingman with his despairing wife and children. The works of

Gustave Doré, Adolphe Felix Cals, Constantin Meunier, and Jean-François Raffaëllé, in France, also provide interesting comparisons. See Linda Nochlin, *Realism* (Baltimore, 1972).

5. In this respect it is tempting to speculate on a possible connection between Grinager and the Spanish artist Joaquin Sorolla y Bastida. Sorolla's paintings were known in America from 1893 when he exhibited a much-admired painting, *Another Marguerite*, at the Chicago Exposition to 1909 when a one-man exhibition of his work was held at the Hispanic Society of America in uptown New York. His picture *Sad Inheritance* of 1899 (eventually given to the Church of the Ascension, New York) is particularly relevant to Grinager. It shows a group of nude and crippled boys being helped by a priest to enjoy a romp in the sea. The somberness of the theme is alleviated by the sparkling effect of bright sunlight on the sea and by the open air. Although Sorolla's painting postdates Grinager's by five years, it is intriguing as a contemporary artist's use of a spontaneous, impressionistic technique to comment on the human condition. See Priscilla E. Muller, "Sorolla in America," *American Artist*, April, 1974, pp. 22ff.

6. A letter from Luther Ford (dated March 17, 1970) to the Fidelity Bank and Trust Company of Minneapolis, which reproduced the painting in its *Progress Report* of 1969, identifies the old structures in the painting.

Appendix: Painters and Sculptors Associated with Minnesota, 1820–1914

Appendix
*Painters and Sculptors
Associated with Minnesota, 1820–1914*

This first attempt to list artists who have created works with a Minnesota association gives the life dates whenever possible. In many cases little additional information concerning these artists is available. No attempt has been made to differentiate between amateur and professional artists.

The best sources for this material are Donald R. Torbert, *A Century of Art and Architecture in Minnesota* (Minneapolis, 1958), and the clippings file "Art and Artists, Biography" in the Minnesota Historical Society Library. I hope that this beginning will facilitate further research on the subject.

ELLEN W. BAUER

Andrews, S. Holmes. In 1843 living in New York City and exhibiting at the National Academy of Design. Oil painting and lithograph by him of St. Paul (1855), in the collection of the Minnesota Historical Society.

Banvard, John. 1815–1891. Itinerant portrait painter working in the Mississippi and Ohio River valleys in the late 1830's. Painter of "Three Mile Painting" (panorama of the Mississippi) now lost.

Bartlett, ——. New York portraitist and landscapist. Studio in St. Paul in 1863–1864.

Bass, Frank. B. 1848. First artist born in Minnesota. Worked in St. Paul in the 1870's. Made an unsuccessful attempt to start an art school.

Bastian, Huber. 1844–1892. In Rochester in 1867. Sketchbook in Olmsted County Historical Society.

Berndt, J. Lithograph of New Ulm in 1860.

Bierstadt, Albert. 1830–1902. Well-known American landscapist. Born and trained in Düsseldorf. Painter of large, theatrical views of the West.

Bingham, George Caleb. 1811–1879. One of the best known western artists. Studied in Philadelphia, Paris, Düsseldorf. Noted for genre scenes of Missouri life.

Blashfield, Edwin Howland. 1848–1936. Paris-trained leading American mural painter. Painter of *The Fifth Minnesota Regiment at Corinth* in the governor's reception room and two lunettes in the Senate Chamber of the Capitol (c. 1905).

Bradish, Alvah. 1806–1901. National Academy exhibitor. In St. Paul in 1858 and 1876. Minnesota portraits include those of Bishop Henry B. Whipple and Governor Cushman K. Davis.

Brewer, Nicholas R. 1857–1949. Landscape and portrait painter. Received his first commission from Henry Ward Beecher. Portrait of Franklin D. Roosevelt in 1934.

Bricher, Alfred Thompson. 1837–1908. New England artist in Minnesota during summer of 1866. Sketched the Lake Pepin area.

Brill, Ethel. Water-colorist in the early 1900's. Noted author and illustrator of children's books.

Calson, L. Landscape with church (1895) in a private St. Paul collection.

Carling, Henry. 1856–1932. Native of Manchester, England. In St. Paul in 1888. Illustrator, copier of paintings. Executed portraits including those of James J. Hill and Archbishop John Ireland.

Carver, Captain Jonathan. 1732–1780. Led expedition to Minnesota in 1767. Sketched Lake Pepin and the Falls of St. Anthony for his journal.

Catlin, George. 1796–1872. Well-known painter of Indians and the West. Author of monumental work on North American Indian life.

Cawse, John E. Copier of paintings by Peter Rindisbacher.

Christenson, Lars. 1839–1910. Norwegian immigrant woodcarver. Settled in Benson, Minnesota, in 1866. Created altarpiece (1897–1904) for church in Benson.

Clark, Mrs. Sadie Stephens. D. 1899. Wife of a Stillwater doctor. Painted portrait of "Uncle Jim" Carter, in the collection of the Washington County Historical Society.

Clausen, Peter Gui. 1830–1924. Danish-born and trained. Settled in Minneapolis in 1869. Painter of Minneapolis landscapes and of panorama of the West.

Conner, Herbert. Two Herbert Conners known, possibly the same man. S.S. *Manistee* (1897) in the collection of the St. Louis County Historical Society signed Herbert L.(?) Conner. Herbert G. Conner (1851–1933). Newspaper artist for the *St. Paul Globe* in the 1880's. Also portraitist and painter of at least one scene relating to Minnesota history.

Conner, N. Painted logging scene (1885), in private St. Paul collection.

Conway, John Severinus. 1852–1925. Milwaukee sculptor and painter. Educated at Chicago Art Institute. Summer trips in the 1870's to Minnesota to paint landscapes.

Cooley, Ben. Portraitist in St. Paul in the 1850's and 1860's. Resident of Kalamazoo, Michigan, before and after stay in Minnesota.

Cox, Kenyon. 1856–1919. Muralist. Follower of John La Farge. Painter of lunette above the staircase leading to the Supreme Court Chamber in State Capitol.

Cross, Henry. 1877–1918. Portraits of Sioux Indians condemned to death after the New Ulm massacre (1862). Portrait of John Other Day (1863), survivor of massacre aftermath, in The Minneapolis Institute of Arts.

Currier, Nathaniel. 1813–1893. Well-known lithographer with James Merritt Ives (1824–1895). Commissioned a view of Minnehaha Falls.

Dawes, Edwin M. 1872–1934. Born Boone, Iowa. Minneapolis area painter during the early twentieth century, later Nevada and California resident. *Channel to the Mills* (1913) in The Minneapolis Institute of Arts.

Deas, Charles. 1818–1867. Well-known nineteenth-century painter. Traveled west in 1840. Painter of Minnesota scenes in that decade.

Dietel, S. Mentioned in the St. Paul press in 1875 as a carver of figures of saints for churches in the area.

Dufferin and Ava, Marquess of (Frederick Temple Hamilton Blackwood). 1826–1902. Much-traveled diplomat and amateur artist. Painted water colors of Canada and at least one of Minnesota.

Duncanson, Robert S. 1817-22–1872. Well-known black Cincinnati artist. Painted *The Falls of Minnehaha* (1862).

Durran, S. J. Primitive artist in Winona at the turn of the century. Painted *Sunday Afternoon on the Levee* (1895), in the collection of the Winona County Historical Society.

Eastman, Seth. 1808–1875. Commandant of Fort Snelling in the 1840's. Well-known painter of the West. Illustrator of books on Indian life.

Edwards, Elijah E. 1831–1915. Minister, teacher, artist. Spent many years in Taylors Falls. Painted scenes of the St. Croix River.

Eich, Peter. 1834–1920. Stearns County farmer associated with the carpentry shop of St. John's Abbey, Collegeville. Made furniture and shrine for abbey.

Ely, Mrs. Edward. Primitive portraitist working in Winona in the 1870's.

Falkenshield, Dr. Andrew. 1822?–1896. Danish surgeon and artist. Arrived in St. Paul in 1856. Established painting and photography studio.

Fjelde, Jacob H. F. 1855–1896. Danish sculptor. Arrived in Minneapolis in 1887. Several works, including *Minnehaha and Hiawatha*, in Minneapolis and St. Paul parks.

Flagg, Charles Noel. 1848–1916. New York artist in St. Paul in the late 1880's. Painted local portraits. Attempted, unsuccessfully, to establish an art school.

Fleury, Albert. 1848–1924. Born in France, settled in Chicago in 1888, taught at Chicago Art Institute. Murals in Merchants National Bank in Winona. Painting of Farmers National Bank in Owatonna (1914).

Fournier, Alexis Jean. 1865–1948. Minneapolis artist. Studied Minneapolis School of Art and abroad. Many paintings of local scene.

Frazer, James Earle. 1876–1953. Born in Winona, studied at the École des Beaux-Arts, Paris. Sculptor and medalist. Received commission for Indian Head Nickel and statue of Alexander Hamilton at the Treasury Building, Washington, D.C.

French, Daniel Chester. 1850–1931. Nationally known sculptor. Chosen as chief sculptor for State Capitol. Created Capitol's quadriga with Edward C. Potter.

Frisbie, W. H. Minnesota portraitist in the 1880's.

Fuller, George F. 1822–1884. Painter of water-color sketches of Minnesota in 1853, in the collection of the Minnesota Historical Society.

Gág, Anton. 1859–1908. Bohemian immigrant to New Ulm in 1872. Painter of panorama of the New Ulm massacre (1892–1893). Father of Wanda Gág, a well-known illustrator.

Gausta, Herbjørn. 1854–1924. Norwegian immigrant to Minnesota. Studied in Europe. Portraits and landscapes of Minnesota.

Gilbert, Cass. 1859–1934. Architect and project supervisor of the State Capitol at the turn of the century. Architect of Woolworth Building, New York (1913), and Supreme Court Building, Washington, D.C. (1935).

deGornon, Vincent. Portrait painter living in the Minneapolis area in the 1880's.

Grant, Mrs. G. B. Minneapolis–St. Paul area artist in the 1880's. Landscapist of European scenes.

Grinager, Alexander. 1865–1949. Son of Norwegian settlers in Albert Lea. Studied with Peter Clausen in Minneapolis and at Académie Julien in Paris. Did impressionistic paintings of local scene in the 1890's. Later resident of Ossining, N.Y.

Gutherz, Charles (Carl). (Also spelled Guthers.) 1844–1907. Swiss-born artist. Arrived in St. Paul in 1873. Painter of allegorical themes and portraits of governors, including Horace Austin (1873) and Lucius F. Hubbard (1887) in the State Capitol.

Gwynne, Harriet Lee. Pupil of Elijah Edwards. Amateur painter of landscapes and flower pictures in Taylors Falls.

Hall, C. Painter of *View of Ft. Snelling* (1877), in collection of the Minnesota Historical Society.

Hall, William M. *Trout Fisherman* (1867), in the collection of the Minnesota Historical Society.

Harwood, Burt. First director of the St. Paul School of Fine Arts, founded in 1894.

Healy, George Peter Alexander. 1813–1894. Paris-trained portrait painter of international reputation. Portraits of Mr. and Mrs. Henry Rice in the collection of the Minnesota Historical Society.

Healy, Thomas Cantwell. 1820–1873. Brother of George Healy. Also Paris trained. He painted the portrait of Henry H. Sibley in St. Paul in 1857.

Heller, Christian. Worked with Anton Gág and Ignatz Schwendinger in New Ulm, with whom he founded an art school in 1892.

Herrst. Painter of Minneopa Falls, in the collection of the Blue Earth County Historical Society.

Hoeffler, Adolf Johann. 1825–1898. Born in Frankfurt, Germany. Trained at Düsseldorf Academy. In Minnesota in 1849 and again in 1852. Sketches of landscapes in St. Paul–Minneapolis area.

Hoelzlhuber, Franz. 1826–1898. Born in Gruendberg, Austria. Settled in Milwaukee in 1856. Water colors and sketches, for illustrated magazines, of travels in America, including some of the Mississippi. Returned to Austria in 1860.

Holm, Julius. Primitive painter of *Tornado over St. Paul* (1893).

Howe, Jonas Holland. 1821–1898. Politician and farmer in Plymouth, Minnesota. Copier of popular prints and engravings. *The Artist's Paradise* reflects a provincial knowledge of contemporary landscape painting.

Hyde, William Henry. 1858–1943. Paris-trained New York artist. Landscapes of Minnesota in late nineteenth century include a view of Fort Snelling (c. 1890).

Jackson, F. Two water colors (dated 1857), *Ft. Snelling, Upper Mississippi* and *Sioux Encampment, Upper Mississippi*, in the collection of the Minnesota Historical Society.

James, Frances Linda. Water colors by this artist in the collection of the Minnesota Historical Society include *Hexagonal Tower, Ft. Snelling*, and *Minnehaha Falls* (c. 1910).

Johnson, Carl Edward. 1883–1948. Teacher of drawing at the University of Minnesota, lithographer, and etcher. Scenes of Minnesota and Minneapolis, particularly views of bridges and mills.

Johnson, Charles F. Pencil drawing *St. Paul in 1869*, in the collection of the Minnesota Historical Society.

Johnson, Eastman. 1824–1906. Well-known painter from New England. In 1856 and 1857 in Duluth, where he painted landscapes and scenes of Chippewa Indian life.

Kane, Paul. 1810–1871. Canadian painter. Executed *Sioux Scalp Dance* (Royal Ontario Museum, Toronto) depicting Sioux at Fort Snelling and probably a copy of a lost painting.

Kellogg, Harry J. Painter of *Minnesota Regiment at Kelly's Field* (1890), in the collection of the Minnesota Historical Society.

Kensett, John Frederick. 1816–1872. Well-known landscapist of the Hudson River School. In Minnesota in 1854.

Kent, Rockwell. 1882–1971. Pupil of Chase and Henri. Painter and illustrator of scenes of American life. In Winona in 1913.

Klangstad, August. 1866–1949. Norwegian painter living in Minneapolis for thirty-three years. Executed more than 3,000 altarpieces.

Koehler, Robert. 1850–1917. Studied in New York and Munich. Best known work *The Strike* (1886). Second director of the Minneapolis School of Art. Painter and portraitist in Minneapolis (1893–1917).

La Farge, John. 1835–1910. Eclectic painter. Student of Richard Morris Hunt. Influenced by Theodore Chassériau. American mural painter, including lunettes in Supreme Court Chamber in State Capitol.

Larpenteur, James Deverreux. 1847–c. 1915. St. Paul artist. Studied in Europe. Painter of European landscapes and local Twin Cities subjects.

LeDuc, Alice. 1868–c. 1965. Amateur artist in Hastings. C. 1901 water color of Fort Snelling troops near Hastings in the collection of the Minnesota Historical Society.

Lewis, Henry. 1819–1904. English-born artist. In St. Louis in 1836. Author of *Das Illustrierte Mississippithal* published in Düsseldorf (1858). Resident there from

1853 until his death. Illustrations in book based on his panorama. Painter of many Minnesota landscapes of the 1840's and 1850's.

Lewis, James Otto. 1799–1858. Portraits of Indians at Treaty of Prairie du Chien. Copies appear in *The Aboriginal Portfolio* (1835).

Loemans, Alexander F. Active 1864–1894. Popular landscapist of Minneapolis–St. Paul area in the 1870's. Possibly born in France. St. Anthony resident 1873–1880. Subsequent travel to Far West, Canada, South America.

Lowry, Mrs. James J. Primitive artist. Painter of scenes of Beaver Bay, Minnesota. Wife of local school teacher.

von Luerzer, Feodor. 1851–1913. Austrian-born artist. In Duluth 1889–1909. Painter of many logging scenes and landscapes.

Lund, Peter F. D. 1902. Norwegian-born. In Minneapolis in late 1880's, Duluth in early 1890's. Exhibited *Moonlight on Lake Superior* at the National Academy of Design in New York in 1897. Many landscapes of Duluth and North Shore area.

McAleavy, Michael. Primitive artist of *St. Columkill's Catholic Church in Belle Creek* (c. 1900), in the collection of the Goodhue County Historical Society.

McGrew, Sergeant James G. D. 1907. Primitive artist. Painted *Fort Ridgely, Minnesota* (1890), depicting the burning of the fort during the Sioux uprising in 1862.

Mairs, Clara. 1878–1963. Little-known St. Paul artist. Works in the collection of the Minnesota Historical Society.

Manship, Paul. 1885–1966. Well-known sculptor. Born and studied in St. Paul. Winner of American Prix de Rome in 1909. Best known work *Prometheus Fountain*, Rockefeller Center, New York (1934).

Martin, Homer Dodge. 1836–1897. Well-known landscapist. Influence of French Barbizon School evident in *Harp of the Winds: View of the Seine*, painted in Minnesota in 1896.

Mayer, Frank Blackwell. 1827–1899. Pupil of Alfred Jacob Miller, of Baltimore. In Minnesota in 1851 to observe the signing of the Treaty of Traverse des Sioux. Journal and sketchbooks of Minnesota visit in Newberry Library, Chicago.

Meeker, Joseph Rusling. 1827–1887. Educated at the National Academy, New York. Settled in St. Louis in 1859. Painter of many Mississippi River landscapes. Minnesota views include *Minnehaha Falls.*

Melvold, Haakon. 1841–1888. Norwegian artist in Minneapolis 1885–1888. Landscape of a Norwegian scene in the collection of the Minnesota Historical Society.

Merrill, Katherine. B. 1876. Born in Milwaukee. Studied in Chicago and London. Primarily an etcher. Painting entitled *Granddaughters of General LeDuc* in Hastings, Minnesota.

Millet, Francis D. 1846–1912. Supervisor of murals for World's Columbian Exposition of 1893 in Chicago. Two paintings for governor's reception room in State Capitol.

Momberger, William. 1829–1888? Little-known draftsman. Engraving of *Sugar Loaf Mountain, Winona* in the collection of the Minnesota Historical Society.

Moore, Augustus O. Drawings of Minnesota towns including St. Paul and Stillwater (1863) in the collection of the Minnesota Historical Society.

Munger, Gilbert Davis. 1837–1903. In Minnesota in the 1860's and 1870's. Influenced by French Barbizon School during residence near Barbizon in the 1880's. Several landscapes of Minnesota scenes.

O'Brien, George. Painter of pastel portrait of Marion Donnelly Woltman (1898), former wife of Ignatius Donnelly, in the collection of The Minneapolis Institute of Arts.

Palmer, R. Painted a portrait of Augustus Goodrich in the collection of the Minnesota Historical Society.

Pillsbury, S. His *View of Minnehaha Falls*, dated 1877, is in the Hennepin County Historical Society.

Pomarede, Leon D. c. 1807–1892. French landscape artist and mural painter. Executed *Panorama of the Mississippi River and Indian Life*, exhibited in St. Louis in 1849.

Post, Charles William. 1854–1914. Etcher of scenes in the St. Paul–Minneapolis area, including Fort Snelling (c. 1880) in the collection of the Minnesota Historical Society.

Potter, Edward C. 1857–1923. Animal and equestrian sculptor. Assisted Daniel Chester French with sculpture for State Capitol.

Powie, Robert. Rochester marble cutter. Exhibited bust of General Ulysses S. Grant at local fair.

Pratt, Willis H. B. 1834. Lithographer. In 1871 surgeon at the state prison, Stillwater. Representative in state legislature in 1882. Lithographs include one of Lincoln issuing Proclamation of Emancipation (c. 1865).

Pringle, George W. Hastings, Minnesota, artist. Works include drawing of wife and daughter (1860's).

Pyle, Howard. 1853–1911. Noted illustrator of children's books and American history books. Painter of *Battle of Nashville*, in the governor's reception room in the State Capitol.

Reichardt, Ferdinand. 1819–1895. Danish landscape painter. Exhibited at the National Academy of Design in New York in 1858. Best known for paintings of Niagara Falls. *St. Anthony Falls* in the collection of the Minnesota Historical Society.

Rein, John A. Carpenter and primitive painter of altarpieces, including one depicting the Last Supper for the Rose Church in Old Greenbush, near Roseau, Minnesota (1895).

Resler, George. 1883–1954. Graphic and commercial artist. Executed views of St. Paul before and after the First World War.

Rindisbacher, Peter. 1806–1834. Born in Switzerland. Settled in the Red River colony near Winnipeg in 1821. Painter of Indian life in Manitoba, Dakota, Minnesota, and Wisconsin territories in the 1820's. Died in St. Louis.

Roberts, M. Emma. Supervisor of art in the Minneapolis Public Schools. Water color entitled *Hexagonal Tower and Commissary at Ft. Snelling* (1888) in the collection of the Minnesota Historical Society.

Roos, May. c. 1871–1961. Daughter of Oscar Roos. Born in Taylors Falls. Studied in St. Paul. Executed portraits and landscapes of area.

Roos, Oscar. 1827–1896. Swedish immigrant painter in Taylors Falls.

Rossiter, Thomas Prichard. 1818–1871. Landscape and history painter. Studied in Europe. Influenced by Asher B. Durand and the Hudson River School. *Minnesota Prairie* (1865) in the collection of the University of Minnesota Gallery.

Salisbury, Jonathan B. 1824–1901. Meeker County surveyor. Executed drawings of forts, including those of Fort Ripley and Fort George (1863) in the collection of the Minnesota Historical Society.

Satory, George. B. 1867. Painter and decorator of churches, including the Church of the Assumption in St. Paul (1891) and St. John the Baptist in Jordan.

Schwendinger, Alex. Son of Ignatz Schwendinger. Worked with father on cherub panels for art school in New Ulm. Paintings of Columbus and the New Ulm massacre in the collection of the City Museum and Brown County Historical Society, New Ulm.

Schwendinger, Ignatz. 1831–1904. Austrian sculptor and painter. Settled in New Ulm in 1879. Worked with Heller and Gág on cherub panels for art school. Executed portraits of local people.

Sederberg, Alfred. Two identical views of Winona in 1867, one signed Sederberg. Probably the Alfred Sederberg listed in Minneapolis city directory of 1871–1872.

Sencerbox, Alice Hines. Shakopee artist. *View of Minnehaha Falls* (1870's) in the collection of the Minnesota Historical Society.

Seymour, Samuel. 1796–1823. Painter and engraver. In Philadelphia in 1801. In Minnesota in 1823 with Major Stephen H. Long's expedition. Sketches for expedition include *Indian Encampment at Big Stone Lake, Head of the St. Peter.*

Shaw, Joshua. 1770–1850. Engraved *Falls of St. Anthony on the Mississippi* (c. 1820).

Sloan, J. R. Primitive artist. *St. Anthony Falls* (1856) in the collection of the Minnesota Historical Society.

Sperry, John T. Primitive painter of views. *Homer, Minnesota* (c. 1869) and *Barn Bluff, Red Wing* in the collection of the New York State Historical Society, Cooperstown, N.Y.

Sprague, Howard Freeman. 1871–1899. Painter of whalebacks at Duluth, including one entitled *Whaleback Loading Ore at the Duluth Ore Docks* (1893) in the collection of the St. Louis County Historical Society, Duluth.

Stanley, John Mix. 1814–1872. Portrait painter in Detroit and Chicago. At Fort Snelling in 1839, in St. Paul in 1853. Member of Isaac Stevens's Pacific railroad survey. Drawings of St. Paul–Minneapolis included in survey.

Stenstrom, Andrew Manuel. 1880–1953. Primitive painter of logging camps 1901–1917. Itinerant evangelist and painter of religious subjects and landscapes in Bemidji area.

Stenwick, Albert H. Olson. Red Wing potter. Produced clay figurines entitled *Lady Imnaha* and *The Potter* (1897) and bust of General William Colvill, in the collection of the Goodhue County Historical Society.

Stevens, John. 1816–1879. Self-taught painter. Settled in Rochester in 1853. Painter of panoramas of Sioux massacre.

Strobel, Max. Lithographer of *City of St. Paul* (1853), in the collection of the Minnesota Historical Society. Accompanied Stevens's Pacific railroad survey (1853) as a draftsman.

Sully, General Alfred. 1820–1879. Son of the well-known portrait painter Thomas Sully. Career army officer. Illustrated four Minnesota scenes included in an army report of midwestern forts (1856).

Sussmilch, William A. Painter of *Logging Scene in Minnesota* (1889) when resident of Duluth.

Sweeny, Robert Ormsby. 1831–1902. Commissioned by Minnesota Historical Society to represent flowers and plants of Minnesota and Indian artifacts.

Thomas, Sergeant Edward K. 1817–1906. Philadelphia native. At Fort Snelling 1849–1851. Painter of views of the fort. Later resident of Detroit and professional artist.

Thompson, Jerome B. 1814–1886. Born in Middleborough, Massachusetts, to family of artists. Portrait, genre, and landscape painter. View of Minnehaha Falls (1870).

Thorp, Colonel Freeman. 1844–1922. Army colonel. Born in Geneva, Ohio. In Crow Wing County in 1895. Received government commissions for portraits of national figures, including Lincoln and Grant. Painter of murals for court house, Brainerd.

Volk, Douglas. 1856–1935. Son of sculptor Leonard Volk. Studied in Italy and Paris. 1886–1893 first director of Minneapolis School of Art. Painter of local portraits and genre scenes.

Walker, James. 1819–1899. Copier of Catlin paintings. Received commissions for paintings of Civil War battles, including one entitled *General LeDuc at the Battle of Lookout Mountain* now in Hastings.

Ward, Jacob C. 1809–1891. East coast artist. In early 1840's painted Minnesota landscapes, including *Lake Pepin, Upper Mississippi* and *The Soaking Mountain on the Upper Mississippi.*

Washburn, Cadwallader L. 1866–1965. Minnesota artist. Member of prominent milling family. Etcher, painter, and journalist.

Weide, John A. B. 1844. Studio in St. Paul. *View of St. Paul from East 7th St.* (1893) in the collection of the Minnesota Historical Society.

Wellge, H. Lithograph entitled *Panoramic View of Lake Benton, Minnesota* (1883) in the collection of the Minnesota Historical Society.

White, J. Chester. Born in Ireland. In Minnesota by 1865. Pencil drawing of Fort Ridgely (1866) in the collection of the Minnesota Historical Society. Later a merchant in Waseca and representative in state legislature.

Whitefield, Edwin. 1816–1892. English-born landscape painter. In New York in 1840. In Minnesota 1855–1860. St. Paul and Minneapolis included in volume of lithographs of North American cities. Executed promotional water colors for real estate ventures in Kandotta and other Minnesota areas.

Whitefield, Wilfred J. D. 1926. Son of Edwin Whitefield. Lithograph entitled *View of Sauk Centre, Minnesota 1868* in the collection of the Minnesota Historical Society.

Whitney, Frank. 1860–1935. Student of Bouguereau in Paris. Illustrator for *The Horseman* (Chicago). *Equine Aristocracy* (1889) in the collection of the Olmsted County Historical Society in Rochester.

Wild, John Caspar. c. 1806–1846. Swiss-born artist in Minnesota in 1844.

Wimar, Carl. 1828–1862. St. Louis artist. Düsseldorf-trained painter of dramatic scenes of Indian life. In Minnesota in 1849 as assistant to Leon Pomarede.

Winnen, Peter. Mentioned in the St. Paul press in 1864 as a carver of a gravestone decorated with lettering and symbols.

Wood, Thomas Waterman. 1823–1903. Pupil of Chester Harding in Boston. Known for genre scenes. Painter of Little Crow at Fort Snelling (1862), in The Minneapolis Institute of Arts.

Zogbaum, Rufus F. 1849–1925. Painter of *Battle of Gettysburg* (c. 1905) in the governor's reception room in the State Capitol.

Selected Bibliography

Books

Bergman, Peter. *American Art in the Barbizon Mood.* Washington, D.C., 1975.

Blegen, Theodore C. *Grass Roots History.* Minneapolis, 1947.

Blegen, Theodore C. *Minnesota: A History of the State.* Minneapolis, 1963.

Bloch, Maurice. *George Caleb Bingham: A Catalogue Raisonné.* 2 vols. Berkeley, Calif., 1967.

Catlin, George. *North American Indians, Being Letters and Notes on Their Manners, & Customs, Written during Eight Years Travel amongst the Wildest Tribes of Indians in North America,* 2 vols. London, 1841.

Craven, Wayne. *Sculpture in America.* New York, 1968.

Cresson, Margaret French. *Journey into Fame: The Life of Daniel Chester French.* Cambridge, Mass., 1947.

Cummings, Frederick, and Allen Staley. *Romantic Art in Britain: Painting and Drawing, 1760–1860.* Philadelphia, 1968.

Curry, Lawrence. *The American West: Painters from Catlin to Russell.* Exhibition Catalogue. New York, 1972.

Eastman, Mary H. *Dahcotah; or, Life and Legends of the Sioux around Fort Snelling.* Illustrated from drawings by Captain Eastman. New York, 1849.

Ewers, John C. *Artists of the Old West.* Garden City, N.Y., 1965.

Folwell, William Watts. *A History of Minnesota.* 4 vols. St. Paul, 1921.

Gerdts, William H. *American Neo-Classic Sculpture: The Marble Resurrection.* New York, 1973.

Groce, George C., and David H. Wallace. *The New York Historical Society's Dictionary of Artists in America, 1564–1860.* New Haven, Conn., 1966.

Harris, Neil. *The Artist in American Society: The Formative Years 1790–1860.* New York, 1966.

Heilbron, Bertha L. *Making a Motion Picture in 1848.* St. Paul, 1936.

Heilbron, Bertha L. *With Pen and Pencil on the Frontier in 1851.* St. Paul, 1932.

Heilbron, Bertha L., editor. Introduction to *The Valley of the Mississippi Illustrated,* by Henry Lewis. Trans. A. Hermina Poatgieter. St. Paul, 1967.

High Museum of Art, the. *The Düsseldorf Academy of the Americans.* Atlanta, 1972.

Hills, Patricia. *The American Frontier: Images and Myths.* New York, 1973.

Hills, Patricia. *Eastman Johnson.* New York, 1972.

Hills, Patricia. *The Painters' America: Rural and Urban Life, 1810–1910.* New York, 1974.

Hoopes, Donelson. *American Narrative Painting.* Los Angeles, 1974.

Howatt, John K. *The Hudson River School and Its Painters.* New York, 1972.

Howatt, John K. *John Frederick Kensett, 1816–1872.* New York, 1968.

Josephy, Alvin M. *The Artist Was a Young Man: The Life Story of Peter Rindisbacher.* Fort Worth, Tex., 1970.

Kinietz, W. Vernon. *John Mix Stanley and His Indian Paintings.* Ann Arbor, Mich., 1942.

Larkin, Oliver W. *Art and Life in America.* New York, 1964.

Leach, Frederick D. *Paul Howard Manship.* St. Paul, 1968.

McCracken, Harold. *Portrait of the Old West*. New York, 1952.

McDermott, John Francis. *Lost Panoramas of the Mississippi*. Chicago, 1968.

McDermott, John Francis. *Seth Eastman: Pictorial Historian of the Indian*. Norman, Okla., 1961.

McDermott, John Francis. *Seth Eastman's Mississippi: A Lost Portfolio Recovered*. Urbana, Ill., 1973.

McLanathan, Richard. *The American Tradition in the Arts*. New York, 1968.

Murtha, Edwin. *Paul Manship*. New York, 1957.

Novak, Barbara. *American Painting of the Nineteenth Century*. New York, 1969.

Osborn, Chase S., and Stellanova Osborn. *Schoolcraft, Longfellow, Hiawatha*. Lancaster, Pa., 1942.

Parry, Elwood. *The Image of the Black Man and the Indian in American Art, 1590–1900*. New York, 1974.

Rathbone, Perry T., ed. *Westward the Way*. St. Louis, 1954.

Richardson, E. P. *Painting in America from 1502 to the Present*. New York, 1965.

Sweet, Frederick A. *The Hudson River School and the Early American Landscape Tradition*. New York, 1945.

Taft, Robert. *Artists and Illustrators of the Old West*. New York, 1953.

Taliaferro, Lawrence. *Journals*. On microfilm. Minnesota Historical Society, St. Paul.

Thompson, Neil B. *Minnesota's State Capitol: The Art and Politics of a Public Building*. St. Paul, 1974.

Torbert, Donald R. *A Century of Art and Architecture in Minnesota*. Minneapolis, 1958.

Tuckerman, Henry F. *Book of the Artists: American Artists Life: Comprising Biographical and Critical Sketches of American Artists: Preceded by a Historical Account of the Rise and Progress of Art in America*. New York, 1867.

Journal Articles

Bushnell, David I., Jr. "John Mix Stanley, Artist-Explorer," *Annual Report*, Smithsonian Institution, 3(1924): 507–512.

Christianson, Theodore. "The Long and Beltrami Explorations in Minnesota One Hundred Years Ago," *Minnesota History*, November, 1923, pp. 249–285.

Coen, Rena N. "Edward K. Thomas: Fort Snelling Artist," *Minnesota History*, Fall, 1969, pp. 317–326.

Coen, Rena N. 'The Last of the Buffalo," *American Art Journal*, November, 1973, pp. 83–94.

Ewers, John C. "George Catlin, Painter of Indians and the West," *Annual Report*, Smithsonian Institution, Publication No. 4232, 1955, pp. 483–528.

Geske, Norman. "Jonas Holland Howe, a Pioneer Minnesota Artist," *Minnesota History*, Fall, 1950, pp. 99–104.

Heilbron, Bertha L. "Documentary Panorama," *Minnesota History*, March, 1949, pp. 14–23.

Heilbron, Bertha L. "Edwin Whitefield, Settlers' Artist," *Minnesota History*, Summer, 1966, pp. 62–77.

Heilbron, Bertha L. "Frontier Artists," *American Heritage*, Winter, 1950, pp. 8–13.

Johnson, Lila M. "Found (and Purchased): Seth Eastman Water Colors," *Minnesota History*, Fall, 1971, pp. 258–267.

Kingsbury, David L. "Sully's Expedition against the Sioux, 1864," *Minnesota Historical Society Collections*, 8(1898): 449–462.

McDermott, John Francis. "Charles Deas: Painter of the Frontier," *Art Quarterly*, 13(Autumn, 1950):293–311.

McDermott, John Francis. "Peter Rindisbacher, Frontier Reporter," *Art Quarterly*, 12(Spring, 1949):129–144.

Mills, Paul Chadbourne. "The Buffalo Hunter and Other Related Versions of the Subject in Nineteenth Century Art and Literature," *Archivero I*, 1973, pp. 131–172.

Nelson, Marion J. "Herbjørn Gausta, Norwegian-American Painter," *Studies in Scandinavian-American Interrelations*, 1971, pp. 1–24.

Nelson, Marion J. "A Pioneer Artist and His Masterpiece," *Norwegian-American Studies*, 1965, pp. 3–17.

Porter, James A. "Robert S. Duncanson, Midwestern Romantic-Realist," *Art in America*, October, 1951, pp. 98–153.

Rowland, Benjamin. "Popular Romanticism: Art and the Gift Books," *Art Quarterly*, 20(Winter, 1957):364–381.

Wilson, Clifford. "Peter Rindisbacher, First Western Artist," *Canadian Art*, 20(January, 1963):50–53.

Woodall, Allen E. "William Joseph Snelling and the Early Northwest," *Minnesota History*, December, 1929, pp. 367–385.

Index

Index